Otto Gunter

Angelic Channeling
The Art of Receiving Celestial Guidance

Original Title: Angelic Channeling - The Art of Receiving Celestial Guidance

Copyright © 2025, published by Luiz Antonio dos Santos ME.

This book is a non-fiction work that explores practices and concepts in the field of spiritual connection and angelic communication. Through a comprehensive approach, the author offers practical tools to develop sensitivity, align personal vibration, and receive guidance from celestial beings.

1st Edition

Production Team

Author: Otto Gunter
Editor: Luiz Santos
Cover: Studios Booklas/ *Evelyn Harper*
Consultant: *Thomas Wren*
Researchers: *Carmen Ellis*, *Jonathan Hayes*, *Alicia Moore*
Layout: *Richard Keane*

Publication and Identification

Angelic Channeling - The Art of Receiving Celestial Guidance
Booklas, 2025
Categories: Spirituality / Personal Development
DDC: 133.9 - CDU: 133.72
All rights reserved to:
Luiz Antonio dos Santos ME / Booklas

No part of this book may be reproduced, stored in a retrieval system, or transmitted in any form — electronic, mechanical, photocopying, recording, or otherwise — without prior written permission from the copyright holder.

Summary

Sistematic Index 5
Prologue 9
Chapter 1 The Call of Light 12
Chapter 2 Angels and the Celestial Choirs 17
Chapter 3 How Do Angels Speak? 24
Chapter 4 Body, Mind, and Soul 31
Chapter 5 Creating Your Angelic Sanctuary 39
Chapter 6 Chakras in Channeling 46
Chapter 7 Connection Tools 53
Chapter 8 Personal Vibration 60
Chapter 9 Prayers and Invocations 67
Chapter 10 Feeling the Angelic Presence 74
Chapter 11 Clearing Energy Blocks 81
Chapter 12 Expanded Sensitivity 88
Chapter 13 Personal Angels and Universal Angels 95
Chapter 14 The Golden Link 103
Chapter 15 Altered States and Subtle Trance 111
Chapter 16 Recording Contacts 118
Chapter 17 Angelic Symbols and Signatures 125
Chapter 18 Personal Angelic Name 132
Chapter 19 Channeled Writing 139
Chapter 20 Inner Voice and Angelic Voice 146
Chapter 21 Trials and Tests of the Channel 153
Chapter 22 Working with the Circle of Angels 160

Chapter 23 Tuning in with Specific Archangels 167
Chapter 24 Channeling Angelic Names and Seals 175
Chapter 25 Sounds and Frequency Codes 182
Chapter 26 The Channel's Mission 189
Chapter 27 The First Complete Channeling 195
Chapter 28 From Channel to Instrument 203
Chapter 29 Manifesting the Angelic Alliance 209
Epilogue 216

Sistematic Index

Chapter 1: The Call of Light - Explores the subtle call to connect with angels, a universal invitation to experience the presence of these beings of light.

Chapter 2: Angels and the Celestial Choirs - Delves into the celestial hierarchy of angels, from Seraphim to Angels, describing their roles and unique vibrational signatures.

Chapter 3: How Do Angels Speak? - Explores the subtle language of angels, which transcends words and manifests through sensations, images, and synchronicities.

Chapter 4: Body, Mind, and Soul - Explains the importance of aligning the body, mind, and soul to create a clear and receptive channel for angelic communication.

Chapter 5: Creating Your Angelic Sanctuary - Guides the reader through creating a physical and vibrational sanctuary to facilitate connection with angels.

Chapter 6: Chakras in Channeling - Discusses the role of chakras as energy centers and portals for receiving and translating angelic frequencies.

Chapter 7: Connection Tools - Explores various tools, such as crystals, candles, and symbols, that can aid in attuning to angelic frequencies.

Chapter 8: Personal Vibration - Emphasizes the importance of aligning personal vibration with the frequency of love to facilitate communication with angels.

Chapter 9: Prayers and Invocations - Explores the power of prayers and invocations as vibrational expressions that connect us with the angelic realm.

Chapter 10: Feeling the Angelic Presence - Describes the subtle ways in which we can perceive the presence of angels, through sensations, emotions, and inner knowing.

Chapter 11: Clearing Energy Blocks - Guides the reader through identifying and clearing energy blocks that hinder angelic communication.

Chapter 12: Expanded Sensitivity - Discusses the development of expanded sensitivity, including clairvoyance, clairaudience, and claircognizance, to perceive the subtle dimensions.

Chapter 13: Personal Angels and Universal Angels - Explores the distinction between personal angels who accompany us throughout our lives and universal angels who assist us in specific moments.

Chapter 14: The Golden Link - Explores the golden link, the energetic connection between our soul and the angelic realm, and how to strengthen it.

Chapter 15: Altered States and Subtle Trance - Guides the reader through entering an altered state of consciousness, a subtle trance, to facilitate angelic communication.

Chapter 16: Recording Contacts - Emphasizes the importance of recording angelic contacts to deepen the connection and track personal transformation.

Chapter 17: Angelic Symbols and Signatures - Explores the use of symbols and energetic signatures as a direct form of communication with angels.

Chapter 18: Personal Angelic Name - Discusses the significance of receiving and recognizing the name of your personal guardian angel.

Chapter 19: Channeled Writing - Explains the practice of channeled writing, where the channel serves as a direct instrument for angelic communication.

Chapter 20: Inner Voice and Angelic Voice - Guides the reader in discerning between their own inner voice and the subtle voice of angels.

Chapter 21: Trials and Tests of the Channel - Explores the challenges and trials that channels may face on their journey and how to overcome them.

Chapter 22: Working with the Circle of Angels - Discusses the concept of a personal circle of angels and how to connect with and receive guidance from this spiritual team.

Chapter 23: Tuning in with Specific Archangels - Provides guidance on how to connect with and receive support from specific archangels, such as Michael, Raphael, and Gabriel.

Chapter 24: Channeling Angelic Names and Seals - Explores the advanced practice of channeling angelic names and seals to deepen the connection and access higher frequencies.

Chapter 25: Sounds and Frequency Codes - Delves into the subtle realm of sounds and frequency codes as a primordial language of angelic communication.

Chapter 26: The Channel's Mission - Discusses the channel's mission to serve as a bridge between the angelic realm and the human world, expressing light and wisdom in their own unique way.

Chapter 27: The First Complete Channeling - Guides the reader through preparing for and experiencing their first complete channeling session, marking a significant step in their spiritual journey.

Chapter 28: From Channel to Instrument - Explores the transformation from being a channel to becoming a true instrument of light, integrating angelic wisdom and love into all aspects of life.

Prologue

Do not underestimate the synchronicity that brought you here. Every encounter with a book like this is a whisper from a greater intelligence, a silent voice echoing in the background of your existence. This is not an invitation to blind belief, but to living experience. More than understanding, you will be called to feel, to cross the veil that separates the visible from the invisible, and to recognize that, from the beginning, there are presences around—and within you—waiting only for you to remember how to hear them.

As you read these pages, you will not just be absorbing ideas or techniques; you will be touching a specific frequency. It is like tuning into a forgotten station, whose ancestral melodies have echoed for millennia in the depths of your being. This book does not teach something new—it awakens what has always been dormant. The art of channeling angelic beings is not a privilege of extraordinary mediums or occult initiates. It is the art of recognizing that you are already a living bridge between heaven and earth. And the words contained here are like gusts of wind gently pushing open the door that separates you from what has always been yours.

Allow yourself to doubt, if you wish. Doubt is not an enemy—it is a guardian that protects what is most sacred in you. But do not allow that same doubt to paralyze you. Every time your mind questions, your heart will feel. Every time logic resists, a gentle memory—one of those that have no clear origin, but bring inexplicable comfort—will touch your skin, like a warm breeze on an autumn morning. What you are about to experience is not a reading, but a crossing. A subtle dive into the invisible web that intertwines your soul with the gentle, constant voice of those who have accompanied you since before your first breath.

The text that inhabits these pages is not a technical manual or a rigid doctrine. It is an echo. A textual reflection of a much older dialogue, held between your spirit and luminous consciousnesses that silently support your journey. Each word is a drop of condensed light, a note of that song that cradles your essence since time immemorial. Each exercise, each proposed reflection, is a gap opened for the angelic presence, always close, to become as palpable as your own breathing.

If you feel, even faintly, that there is something beyond the routine, something lurking through the veils of everyday reality, then this book is a direct invitation to you. It did not come to convince you of anything, because deep down you already know. It came to remember. To echo in the space between your thoughts and emotions that gentle call that you have been pretending not to hear for so long.

This book is a journey of return, and the angels, who reveal themselves within it, are not distant characters. They are intimate soul companions. They are parts of the same creative breath that animates you and that pulsates in every cell of yours. What you will find here are not just stories or theories—they are mirrors. Vibrational mirrors that return to you your own spiritual image, free from dogmas, free from guilt, and free from the veil that has covered your inner vision for so long.

With each chapter, you will be guided beyond the words. You will feel. And by feeling, you will recognize that the connection is not external. It is intimate, organic, inseparable from your essence. The angels will not come from outside, like divine visitors. They will emerge from within, like awakened memories, like forgotten aspects of your own light.

This is a book to be lived, not just read. Each page is a door. Each reflection, a key. And each moment of silence between one paragraph and another, an opportunity for the angelic presence to envelop you, remind you, realign you with the simple and powerful truth: you have never been alone.

If you have come this far, something in you has already answered the call. Allow yourself. Awaken. Cross over.

The invisible waits, patiently, for your first conscious step. This reading is that step.

And the angels—those who already know every beat of your heart—await, with open wings, your return.

Luiz Santos

Editor.

Chapter 1
The Call of Light

There are moments when a gentle restlessness takes hold of us. It is as if, between daily tasks, responsibilities, and the noises of the world, something or someone calls us from within. It is not a voice that echoes in the ears, but a silent sensation that runs through the body and soul, as if a distant memory were trying to emerge. This is the first whisper of angelic channeling: the call of light.

Since ancient times, angels have been described as messengers of the divine, beings who inhabit between planes and whose invisible wings touch the human heart in times of greatest need. No matter the religious, cultural, or spiritual belief—the angelic presence transcends borders, reaching every soul that makes room to feel. But what few know is that this communication is not a privilege of isolated saints or mystics. It is a latent ability in all of us.

Channeling angels is not just hearing words or capturing visions. Before that, it is perceiving the call. A call that arises in moments of silence, when the mind tires of fighting and the heart is willing to listen. It can come after a loss, during a life transition, or even for no apparent reason, just as a breath of longing for something you cannot name.

This longing is the memory that you do not walk alone. It is the echo of your spiritual origin, where you already knew the presence of angels as soul companions. We all, on some level, have walked alongside them, before taking this human form and diving into the density of matter. Angelic channeling is not a novelty; it is a recollection.

Many imagine that channeling is an extraordinary ability, something restricted to mediums, seers, or people with special gifts. But the truth is much simpler and, at the same time, much deeper: channeling is returning to the natural state of connection with light. Before distractions, before masks and emotional defenses, there was a simple clarity. A natural trust that we are supported.

You do not need to be perfect, or spiritually elevated, to feel or channel your angels. It is not a matter of merit. Angels do not judge us, nor choose whom to serve. They are pure emanation of divine love, and divine love does not select. Divine love embraces.

For some, the call of light is subtle—an unexpected interest in spiritual themes, a recurring dream with a luminous presence, or an inexplicable feeling of warmth in the chest. For others, it arrives like a storm: a personal crisis, an illness, an abrupt loss that dismantles all certainties and invites them to seek solace beyond the visible.

Whether subtle or intense, this call is not an accident. It is a response to your soul, which silently asked for help. At some point—consciously or unconsciously—you made a prayer, asked for clarity, protection, direction. And the universe responded, sending signs and opening this channel.

Channeling angels is creating a conscious bridge between your being and the subtle plane where angels vibrate. It is allowing their messages, energies, healings, and teachings to flow to you without filters of the rational mind. It is different from common intuition, as it involves two-way communication—you not only receive insights, but can ask, dialogue, and especially feel the living presence of these beings of light.

Channeling does not mean abandoning your free will or surrendering your personal power to angels. On the contrary: true channeling strengthens who you are, as it reveals your divine essence and your greater purpose. Angels do not come to make decisions for you. They come to illuminate the path, but the step is yours.

Angels do not speak in words, in the human sense. They speak in frequency. Each angel, each archangel, has a unique vibrational signature—a silent melody that resonates directly in your energy field. When you tune into that frequency, words and images arrive as a spontaneous translation of that vibration. Therefore, each channeler perceives the messages differently. There is no right or wrong way, there is only what is true for you.

The first key to opening this channel is simple and challenging: trust what you feel. Even when the mind doubts, even when logic tries to deconstruct, it is in pure feeling that angels reveal themselves.

Many people, when they feel this call, recoil. The fear arises of not being pure enough, of not having adequate spiritual knowledge, or of just fantasizing. This is the greatest block to channeling: the belief that it is necessary to be perfect to receive angels. This is a myth.

Angels are not attracted by perfection, but by sincerity. By the heart willing to make room, even if it is wounded. Often, it is precisely the wounds that create the gaps through which angelic light can enter.

When you accept the call of light, the universe responds immediately. It can be a white feather in your path, an improbable synchronicity, or that sudden feeling that someone is by your side, even with no one visible.

These first signs are invitations. Each small touch is a reminder: you are not alone, you never have been. The veil between the worlds is thin and permeable, and at any moment you can cross it with the force of your intention and your openness.

Each person is called in a unique way. Some hear a sweet and peaceful inner voice. Others feel chills or warmth in their hands. Some see flashes of light or have revealing dreams. It does not matter how the call arrives; what matters is to respond.

The path of angelic channeling is a journey back to yourself. Each message received, each subtle touch, is a piece of the puzzle that reveals who you are beyond name and form. Angels are not outside of you. They are parts of the same light from which you came. Reconnecting with them is, in essence, reconnecting with yourself.

When you feel this call, there is no rigid manual or mandatory ritual. Simply place your hand on your heart, take a deep breath, and say:

"I am ready to listen. Show me the way."

And so, the journey begins.

Chapter 2
Angels and the Celestial Choirs

Angels present themselves as constant and ancestral presences, intertwined with the very history of humanity and the spiritual journey of each soul. They do not appear as distant or mythical figures, but as living consciousnesses that silently accompany every instant of human existence, sustaining the bridge between matter and the divine. Since the dawn of human consciousness, they have inhabited the invisible spaces between worlds, acting as guardians of the cosmic order and as subtle guides to those who, intuitively or by inner calling, seek to reconnect with their own spiritual essence. They are not merely messengers, but extensions of the creative flow itself, silent voices that whisper amidst the turmoil of life and luminous presences that keep the memory of the sacred alive within every human being.

Contact with these angelic hierarchies is not the result of a privilege restricted to a chosen few, but a possibility open to every soul that, with humility and reverence, is willing to cross the dense layers of the mind and ego to recognize the subtlety of the angelic presence. These beings, who fill the spaces between time and eternity, have known each soul since its first emanation of consciousness. They are not strangers, but intimate companions on the journey, silent witnesses to the cycles of learning and awakening. Their messages, though transcending words, resonate directly in the heart, awakening dormant memories and reactivating ancestral codes that connect each soul to its divine origin. This connection, when experienced, dissolves the illusion of separation and reveals that angels are not external beings to be venerated, but mirrors of the divine potentialities that already vibrate latently within each individual.

By understanding the angels and their celestial choirs, it becomes evident that they are not limited to rigid categories or functions, but express living dynamics of service and love in harmony with the need of each instant of the universe. Each choir, each angelic being, carries within it a facet of the original light, adjusted to be accessible to different levels of consciousness. From the flaming and pure presences that directly surround the Source, to the guardian angels who walk alongside each human being, all participate in a single and grand symphony of love and service. Knowing these choirs is not just mapping their functions and hierarchies, but recognizing in each of them a specific vibration that echoes within the human soul itself. By opening oneself to this perception, the seeker not only comes into contact with the angels, but with hidden aspects of himself, understanding that each angelic virtue is also a divine seed dormant in his own heart, awaiting the moment to germinate and blossom in consciousness and sacred action.

Esoteric, as well as theological tradition, tells us of angelic hierarchies. Not as superior and inferior castes, but as concentric circles of function and proximity to the Creator Source. Imagine a great river of light. At the center, the divine presence itself, pure and incandescent. And around this presence, layers and layers of angelic consciousnesses, each vibrating according to its proximity to the origin and its purpose to serve. The closer to the center, the more abstract and subtle these beings are. The closer to humanity, the denser in their light, so that they can be perceived and understood by our limited senses.

Seraphim are described as pure flames. They have no defined form because their essence is the very fire of divine love. They do not speak, because their vibration is so high that their messages are like breaths of consciousness that illuminate without needing words. They are the guardians of the throne, of the original emanation. Being before a seraphim is to experience the dissolution of the ego, the encounter with absolute unity. Therefore, they rarely interact directly with humans. Their function is to keep the primordial flame burning in the heart of the universe.

Next come the cherubim, who have nothing to do with the infantilized image of chubby little angels with bows and arrows. Cherubim are divine intelligence in motion. They are the architects of creation, guardians of universal plans. It is through them that the geometric patterns of existence are sustained. Their messages are complex, full of symbols and codes that the rational mind can barely keep up with. Those who receive messages from cherubim are usually immersed in visions of geometric shapes, living mandalas, light structures that dance in perpetual harmony.

Thrones are living pillars of stability. If cherubim draw the structure, thrones sustain its manifestation. They are the invisible columns that keep the universe upright, anchoring divine light in the foundations of creation. The presence of a throne is felt as a silent and immutable force, like the rock upon which the sea beats without ever moving it. Channeling a throne is receiving the certainty of divine solidity amidst the fluidity of existence.

And then, the choirs closer to human experience begin to emerge. Dominions, responsible for coordinating the actions of angels in specific missions. They are like conductors of an invisible orchestra, ensuring that each note of the divine symphony is played at the right time, in the right tone. Their presence is firm, but loving. They are the ones who teach channels to assume their own power, to take their positions on the grand chessboard of evolution.

Virtues carry within them the energy of miracles. They are conductors of raw divine force, transforming pure intentions into manifest reality. When a human asks for healing, protection, or sincere transformation, it is the virtues that transport that intention from the heart to the divine plane and return the answer in the form of tangible blessings. Their energy is felt as a loving electrical current, a vital impulse that crosses the soul.

Powers are guardians of universal laws. They do not create the laws, but ensure that they are respected at every level of creation. Their presence is implacable, but not cruel. They represent the aspect of divine justice that transcends human morality. Channeling a power is receiving absolute clarity about what is right or wrong for the soul, with no room for doubts or excuses.

And finally, we arrive at the triads closest to us: principalities, archangels and angels. Principalities watch over nations, cultures and large collective movements. They are the weavers of history, inspiring leaders, artists and visionaries to align their actions with the greater plan. Their presence is felt in decisive historical moments, when the destiny of entire peoples is shaped by an inspiration from above.

Archangels are the great intermediaries. Each with their own specialty, they act directly in human life, bringing healing, protection, wisdom, love and direction. Michael, the shield. Raphael, the balm. Gabriel, the voice. Uriel, the flame. Chamuel, the heart. Jophiel, the light of wisdom. Zadkiel, the transmutation. Channeling an archangel is like receiving a discharge of purpose, an activation that rekindles the inner glow and realigns it with the personal mission.

And finally, the angels. Simple, humble, close. They are our invisible companions from birth. The guardian angel, that silent presence that watches over our days and nights, is the first and the last to hold our hand. Channeling your personal angel is like talking to a soul brother who knows us better than we know ourselves. It is hearing gentle, but implacable truths, said with unconditional love.

The celestial choirs, arranged like a ladder of light between the infinite and matter, are not just an ordered hierarchy, but living expressions of the same divine song that echoes throughout existence. Each angelic being carries within it a unique note of this primordial melody, a frequency that not only sustains creation, but invites the human soul to remember its own origin. By recognizing these presences, earthly consciousness expands, realizing that it has never been isolated or lost, but always accompanied by invisible hands that guide, sustain and inspire, even in the most silent and lonely moments.

And it is in this intertwining of vibrations that the human and the divine meet again. Not as opposites, but as parts of the same flow, a single breath of life that folds over itself to know itself through multiple forms. The angels and their choirs do not exist as separate entities, distant in some unattainable heaven, but as mirrors of internal states that rest in the heart of every human being. Knowing them is, in a way, rediscovering oneself, realizing that each angelic virtue already pulsates dormant in every soul, just waiting for the call to awaken.

The journey of connection with angels is not an external search, but an intimate and deep return to what we have always been: divine sparks inhabiting the flesh, learning to remember the forgotten language of light. And when we finally dare to silence the mind and hear this ancestral music, we are filled with the certainty that we have never walked alone. Every step has been accompanied, every fall has been supported, and every prayer, no matter how timid or desperate, has always found attentive ears in the celestial choirs.

Chapter 3
How Do Angels Speak?

Angelic communication reveals itself as a vibrational tapestry that transcends the boundaries of common language, expanding beyond words and penetrating directly into the subtle fields of the human soul. Unlike the linear expectation of the mind, which seeks ordered phrases and direct answers, angels speak through a symphony of sensations, inner images, and sudden intuitions, building a dialogue that transcends intellect and reaches deep layers of consciousness. This form of communication does not obey the sequential logic to which we are accustomed. It manifests as a continuous flow of impressions that, even without a clear verbal form, transmit wisdom, comfort, and direction with a precision impossible to reproduce in words. This celestial language is as old as existence itself, resonating within the soul since before the first incarnation, like an ancestral echo that awaits only inner silence to become audible again.

This angelic language molds itself to the essence of the listener, adapting to the uniqueness of each channel and the individual capacity for spiritual perception. For some, it expresses itself as spontaneous visions—living geometric shapes, landscapes of light, or shining faces that emerge in the inner space of the mind. For others, it manifests as a sudden emotional influx, a wave of tenderness or courage that arises without apparent cause, filling the chest with a silent certainty that a greater presence is near. There are also those who perceive angels through loose words that spring to mind, not as common thoughts, but as fragments of a higher message, laden with a sweetness and clarity that distinguish themselves from any habitual internal monologue. Regardless of the form, the common element is vibration: a unique energetic signature, capable of being felt more than understood, recognized more than explained, which awakens in the soul an intuitive recollection that the presence is familiar, loving, and safe.

In this context, true angelic listening requires an emptying of the mind's noises and a confident surrender to the inner space where the subtle manifests. Angels do not shout, do not impose their messages, and do not compete with the noise of reason anxious for answers. They communicate with the gentleness of a breeze or a light that slips through the crack of a half-open door, offering themselves to the channel without forcing their perception. Therefore, inner silence is the master key to this process. It is in the pause, the recollection, and the serene assent of the soul that their vibrational voices become audible—not with the physical ears, but with the listening of the spiritual heart, which knows how to distinguish the sacred even before the mind understands. Learning this language is, above all, relearning to trust one's own inner senses, rediscovering that the soul has always been fluent in the language of angels and that, more than bringing external messages, these celestial beings awaken the memory of what, deep down, the soul has always known.

Angels do not live in the same rhythm of linear time in which we exist. They flow in layers of reality where past, present, and future intertwine in a single vibrational current. This means that their messages rarely arrive as ordered phrases. Instead, they emerge as impressions, images, feelings, and bursts of sudden understanding that explode within the channel, as if a truth that has always been there were finally recognized. This is the essence of angelic language: truth revealed directly to the heart, without needing to pass through the filter of reason.

When opening oneself to channeling an angel, the first obstacle that arises is doubt. The rational mind, always seeking control and logic, questions whether what is being felt is real or just a figment of the imagination. It is here that many channels interrupt their own connection before it even blossoms. The secret to overcoming this barrier is to understand that angels do not speak just to be heard. They speak to be felt. Their messages are not texts written in the sky; they are vibrations that resonate directly in the most sensitive parts of the soul. Those who learn to trust what they feel open a direct door to the angelic world.

This subtle language often begins with seemingly disconnected signs. A white feather that appears in the path, an unexpected change in the temperature of the environment, a sweet smell in the air without a visible source. Each of these small events is a note in the symphony of communication that angels build around us. They know that our mind needs physical confirmation to believe, so they begin their messages through matter. As the channel learns to recognize these signs, communication deepens.

After the external signs come the internal impressions. A sudden shiver, a warmth that envelops the body, a sudden emotion that does not seem to have a clear origin. Often, the angelic presence is felt as an invisible hug, a wave of peace so intense that words become unnecessary. At these times, what is being said does not matter. What matters is what is being felt—and what is being felt is love. Pure love, without condition, without demand, without restriction.

When the channel becomes familiar with this sensory language, the messages become more specific. They can come in dreams, in spontaneous visions, or even in internal dialogues that arise out of nowhere but carry a wisdom and tenderness that do not resemble the common voice of the mind. The analytical mind doubts, questions, but the heart recognizes. This recognition is the true hallmark of angelic channeling: when you do not need proof because something inside you already knows.

Angels also speak through synchronicity. Those moments when you think of something and, seconds later, see an image or hear a word that confirms exactly that. They take advantage of the cracks in reality to weave messages between the events of your daily life. Not because they need your desperate attention, but because they know you are learning to trust, and each small confirmation reinforces that trust. They speak with the life around you, using the world as a canvas where they paint their answers.

Another essential aspect of angelic language is gentleness. They do not shout. They do not invade. They do not impose themselves. Their presence is like a light touch on a water surface—gentle enough not to scare, but present enough to create ripples that spread. That is why moments of silence are so precious in channeling. It is in silence that the angelic voice becomes audible. Not because it arises from nothing, but because inner stillness allows what has always been there to be perceived.

And there is also the language of inspiration. Often, angels speak in creative impulses, in ideas that spring out of nowhere, in solutions that arise effortlessly. They do not just dictate spiritual messages. They inspire paths, practical answers, decisions that, although they seem common, carry a precision and fluidity that can only come from a higher level of guidance. Creativity, when connected to angelic energy, ceases to be just talent and becomes service—service to one's own spirit and to the greater plan.

Angels also communicate through emotion. Many messages come as waves of pure feeling—love, compassion, peace—that fill the entire inner space of the channel. These messages do not come with words because the feeling itself is the complete communication. In a single instant of absolute love, an angel can transmit more wisdom than pages and pages of text. The challenge is to trust this feeling as a legitimate message, without requiring it to be translated into words.

As the connection deepens, the channel begins to recognize the vibrational signature of each angel. Each being of light has a unique frequency, a "soul tone" that manifests in the body and field of the channel as a specific sensation. Some angels bring warmth, others bring coolness. Some fill the space with golden light, others with a silvery or rosy softness. This signature is their identity, the way they present themselves before they even speak. Over time, the channel learns to identify each presence by how it feels, without needing formal introductions.

Angelic language is alive, fluid, adaptable. It is not a fixed system, but a dance between worlds. Each channel develops their own internal dictionary, their own way of understanding and translating what they receive. There are no absolute rules. What exists is the relationship—intimate, unique, and unrepeatable—between each human soul and the angels that accompany it. Learning this language is relearning to trust one's own feeling, giving back to the soul the right to know what it already knows.

Over time, this dance between worlds becomes a natural extension of one's own consciousness. The channel realizes that they are not just hearing angels but dialoguing with them in a continuous flow, where the separation between sender and receiver dissolves. Messages cease to be isolated events and become part of the daily fabric of life, intertwined in thoughts that arise without explanation, in answers that appear even before the question is asked. And so, the subtle becomes present, and the invisible becomes not just felt but inhabited.

This intimacy built with angels does not arise from the search for ready answers or guarantees of divine protection. It blossoms from the willingness to remain open to mystery, to accept that not every message will come with immediate clarity, and that, often, true communication occurs in layers where words do not reach. It is a relationship of trust and surrender, where the human soul and angelic consciousness learn to recognize each other, not as strangers, but as parts of the same ancestral calling: the calling to remember unity.

And so, the language of angels reveals itself not as a code to be deciphered, but as an invitation to feel life from the inside out. Each sign, each sensation, each shared silence is a reminder that angels do not speak to teach something new, but to awaken what has always been within us. Listening to an angel is, in the end, listening to one's own soul—and discovering that, from the beginning, it was she who taught us to hear.

Chapter 4
Body, Mind, and Soul

The body, mind, and soul form an inseparable triad in the process of angelic channeling, functioning as an integrated network that allows the human being to serve as a bridge between the subtle plane and the physical world. This integration doesn't happen by chance or only at the moment of spiritual connection but is built throughout life, with each choice, care, and perception we cultivate in relation to ourselves. The body is the first foundation of this connection. It is more than a physical vehicle; it is a refined sensory instrument, capable of capturing invisible vibrations and translating them into sensations, intuitions, and even internal visions. The health and state of the body directly influence the clarity of spiritual reception, not because angels depend on physical perfection, but because an intoxicated, rigid, or exhausted body interferes with the natural flow of energy. Bodily harmony, achieved through simple care practices such as conscious breathing, balanced nutrition, and movements that respect one's own rhythm, creates a stable and open base for angelic light to manifest without distortions or blockages.

The mind, in turn, assumes the role of translator and organizer of what the body and soul capture. However, the modern human mind, excessively stimulated, conditioned to linear thinking, and saturated with external information, often becomes a barrier to subtle communication. It tries to interpret spiritual messages with the same mechanisms it uses to solve everyday problems, and this creates noise and distortion. For the mind to fulfill its role without interfering, it needs to be trained to listen in silence, to suspend automatic judgments, and to accept not knowing. This receptive mind is not a blank or passive mind, but a mind refined by the practice of inner silence and by the willingness to welcome subtle impressions without the need to categorize or explain them immediately. It is a mind that learns to live with mystery, to become a servant of the soul, allowing the flow of angelic light and information to express itself with clarity and fluidity.

The soul is the center of this sacred triad. It is the soul that recognizes, before any sign or message, the presence of angels. It vibrates in tune with angelic frequencies because it shares the same divine origin. It is in the soul that the call to channel is born, like a silent recollection that resonates from before the present life. When the body is cared for and the mind silenced, the soul finds the necessary space to express itself without filters. This expression does not come as an external voice, but as an internal recognition—a silent certainty that what is perceived, even without rational explanation, is true. The soul that has been heard and welcomed throughout life, the one that has not been repressed by dogmas or fears, becomes a firm anchor for the angelic presence. It is through the soul that the connection stabilizes and deepens, allowing the human channel to become not just a receiver of messages, but a living presence of light incarnate in the material world.

The harmony between body, mind, and soul is not a distant goal, nor a permanent state of perfection. It is a dynamic process, a daily practice of internal listening and self-care, where each layer of being is recognized as sacred and indispensable. The body is not an obstacle to spirituality; it is the temple where angelic light is anchored. The mind is not an enemy of intuition; it is a tool that, when trained, organizes and gives shape to subtle inspiration. The soul is not a separate entity; it is the divine essence that pulsates in every cell, in every thought, and in every emotion. When these parts learn to dance together, channeling becomes more than an isolated moment of connection. It transforms into a way of living, where the angelic presence ceases to be an occasional visit and becomes a constant companion, flowing in every gesture, thought, and emotion, making the human being themselves a conscious manifestation of divine light on earth.

The body is the foundation of spiritual experience. Although angels are beings of light and do not need a physical body to exist, they can only express themselves in the material world through your body. It is through your senses, your vital energy, your breathing, and even your cells that the angelic presence takes shape and color in the human plane. This means that taking care of the body is not a secondary whim, but an essential part of the channel's preparation. An exhausted, intoxicated, blocked, or constantly suffering body creates interferences that distort the reception of the message. Not because angels shy away from sick bodies, but because the density of bodily suffering creates a fog that hinders the clear translation of light.

Physical perfection is not necessary for channeling. Angels do not demand idealized purity, unrestricted diets, or ascetic practices. But the body needs to be heard, respected, and welcomed. Eating attentively, resting adequately, and allowing vital energy to flow without accumulations or blockages is a form of respect for the channel you are. Physical health, even with its natural imperfections, is a component of spiritual clarity. When you take care of the body, you are telling the universe—and the angels—that you are prepared to sustain the light you wish to receive.

The mind, in turn, is the translator of this light. It is the mind that needs to interpret pure and subtle vibrations and transform them into words, images, and concepts that you understand. But the common mind, accustomed to the constant noise of the world and the hyperactivity of thoughts, is not a reliable translator without preparation. A mind overloaded with worries, anxieties, and limiting beliefs is like a radio tuned to multiple frequencies at the same time—it picks up something here and there, but the result is a jumble of confused sounds.

Preparing the mind for channeling is a process of emptying and refining. It's not about erasing thoughts or forcing artificial silences, but about teaching the mind to take a back seat. The mind needs to learn to serve the soul during channeling, not to control it. This training happens in small daily moments: silencing for a few minutes before starting any practice, observing thoughts without attachment, consciously choosing the content you consume, and avoiding constant mental hyperstimulation. Each small care is like adjusting the antenna so that it picks up only the angelic frequency, and not the noise of the world.

In addition to the body and mind, there is the emotional field. Emotions are the bridge between the visible and the invisible. It is through them that the angelic presence becomes felt, not just perceived intellectually. But repressed emotions, unhealed traumas, and covered pains create dense layers that hinder this perception. Not because angels cannot cross this density, but because pain creates filters that distort what is received. A channel that has not learned to welcome its own emotions will have difficulty distinguishing between an angelic message and a projection of its own needs or fears.

Emotional preparation does not require perfection, but it does require honesty. It is not necessary to "resolve" all pains before channeling, but it is essential to recognize them. Knowing where it hurts, what still bleeds, and what needs healing is a form of internal clarity that avoids confusion during channeling. Angels do not reject wounded channels; on the contrary, they often approach precisely to assist in the healing process. But it is essential that the channel knows how to discern between a message coming from the light and an echo of its own emotional wounds. This discernment is only possible for those who look at themselves with honesty and compassion.

And finally, there is the soul—the true channel. It is from the soul that the call to channeling is born. It is the soul that recognizes angels even before the mind understands or the body feels. The soul already knows each being of light that approaches because it came from the same source from which they emanate. But for the soul to express itself clearly, it needs space. A space free from rigid dogmas, inherited guilt, ancestral fears. The preparation of the soul is a return to its own luminous nature.

This preparation happens in moments of surrender. When you allow yourself to be in silence without expectation, when you open yourself to the angelic presence without demanding proof or guarantees. It is in this state of availability, more than in any elaborate ritual, that the soul aligns with the divine flow. It is not a matter of merit or spiritual conquest, but of sincere availability. The prepared soul is the one that says "yes" without knowing what will come, trusting that whatever presence arrives will bring exactly what is needed.

The body cares for the physical space, the mind organizes and translates, the emotions adjust sensitivity, and the soul guides. When these four layers work in harmony, the channel becomes a clean and safe bridge between the planes. Preparation is not an isolated event before the first channeling; it is a continuous practice.

Each care for the body, each mental pause, each honest look at emotions, and each yes of the soul builds this bridge day after day.

And it is in this intertwining of layers—body, mind, emotions, and soul—that channeling ceases to be just a spiritual practice and becomes a way of existing. Each care, each moment of attention dedicated to one's own being is, in fact, a silent invitation for angelic light to approach effortlessly, because it already finds a prepared space in you. The channel is not an antenna separate from life; it is someone who walks through the world conscious that each gesture of self-care, each inner silence, and each welcomed emotion opens the way for the subtle to reveal itself.

This continuous process of tuning oneself, of adjusting one's own field to be an increasingly clear receptacle, is not a burden or a demand. It is a delicate dance between humanity and the divine, where each part of you is honored and recognized as essential. Angels do not ask for perfection, but they do ask for presence. They want to inhabit a channel that knows itself, that welcomes its shadows without judging itself unworthy, and that understands that the divine manifests precisely in the full acceptance of who one is—light and darkness, heaven and earth.

In the end, preparing to channel angels is preparing to find yourself. There is no real separation between hearing the angelic voice and hearing your own soul, as they are voices that echo from the same source, only in different tones. The whole channel is the one who has learned to silence without fear, to feel without resistance, and to trust without demanding control. In this state of conscious surrender, the body, mind, emotions, and soul become one instrument—and the angelic breath, subtle and loving, can finally pass through every note of this being, transforming it into a living bridge between heaven and earth.

Chapter 5
Creating Your Angelic Sanctuary

Creating an angelic sanctuary is much more than organizing a physical space or decorating a corner of the house with spiritual symbols. It's about building, first and foremost, a vibrational atmosphere capable of welcoming the subtle and elevated presence of angels, allowing their energies to anchor and express themselves fluidly in the material plane. The physical sanctuary, therefore, functions as a tangible mirror of the internal sanctuary, the one that exists in the core of the soul and pulses silently in the center of being. The act of preparing this external space, with intention and love, activates an internal process of alignment, in which body, mind, emotions, and spirit harmonize in the same frequency of receptivity. Each gesture of care, each object positioned, each prayer whispered while preparing the place is, in essence, a conscious invitation for the angels to approach and recognize in that space a point of light amidst the density of the world.

The location chosen for this sanctuary does not need to follow fixed rules, as what truly consecrates it is the intention that permeates it. It can be a small altar on a table, a solitary candle near the bed, or even an outdoor area, where nature actively participates in the subtle vibration one wishes to create. What transforms a common space into an angelic sanctuary is the clarity of purpose: there, between the visible and the invisible, a living bridge between planes is established. More than decoration, each element inserted in the sanctuary carries the energy of personal meaning and the spiritual intention of the one who builds it. The candle is not just a light source, but a symbol of the internal flame that seeks contact with the divine. The crystal is not just a beautiful stone, but an amplifier of vibrations and an anchor of subtle frequencies. The flower is not just an ornament, but a reminder that the ephemeral beauty of matter is a reflection of the eternal harmony of the spirit.

This space, gradually, becomes impregnated with the energy of each encounter, each prayer, each loving silence dedicated to the connection with angels. Just as water absorbs the properties of everything it comes into contact with, the physical environment of the sanctuary absorbs and radiates the vibration of angelic presence and the sincere devotion of those who place themselves there in a state of receptivity. It's a cumulative process: the more love, respect, and reverence are deposited in the space, the more easily it becomes a vibrational anchor, a true beacon for celestial presences. This energetic accumulation creates a unique signature, a kind of luminous portal that transcends the physical and remains active even on days when the space is not consciously used. Angels naturally return to places where they were welcomed with sincerity, as they recognize in these places a familiar vibration, a bridge already built between their spheres and the material world.

Over time, something even deeper happens: the physical sanctuary ceases to be just a fixed point in space and begins to expand within the one who created it. The vibration cultivated there permeates daily gestures, silent thoughts, and even interactions with the external world. The body becomes an extension of the altar, the mind begins to act as a guardian of internal silence, and the heart, now attuned to angelic presence, carries within it the same light that was once lit on the table or in the chosen corner. At this point, the separation between the sacred and the everyday dissolves, and angelic presence ceases to be an occasional visit and becomes a constant companion, flowing in every moment of life. Creating an angelic sanctuary, therefore, is taking the first step towards recognizing that the true sanctuary is you — the living space where heaven and earth meet, and where the divine and the human learn, together, to speak the same language: the language of conscious love.

This sanctuary can be a small altar in a corner of your house, a clean table with a few meaningful objects, or even a chair near a window where sunlight or moonlight can enter. The size or luxury of the space does not matter; what matters is the intention and clarity with which it is prepared. Angels are not attracted by gold or sophisticated ornaments. They are attracted by the purity of intention, the genuine desire for connection, and the love with which every detail is cared for.

Choosing the location is the first act of creation. It doesn't have to be an isolated or removed space from daily life, but it's important that it can be respected as sacred. Even if you share this space with other functions — a table that is also used for study or work, for example — it's your intention to separate that corner as a point of light that transforms it into a sanctuary. Angels are sensitive to human intention. They recognize the loving vibration of those who prepare a space not out of obligation, but out of love for the encounter.

Cleaning the space is the next step. But here, cleaning is not just sweeping or dusting. Cleaning is removing the density accumulated over time — thoughts, arguments, tensions that have impregnated the environment. A simple lit candle with intention, a soft incense, or even a spontaneous prayer made from an open heart is enough to dissolve these layers. Angels do not demand material perfection, but they need a space where vibration can flow freely.

When preparing the sanctuary, symbolic objects become bridges between worlds. Crystals, images, candles, flowers, feathers, or sacred symbols that resonate with your heart are welcome. Each object placed there should carry a story, an intention, or a personal meaning. It's not about decorating the space for the sake of decoration, but about building a symbolic landscape that reflects your personal call to light. Each chosen crystal, each placed flower, each positioned image is a silent invitation for angels to manifest themselves.

Angels recognize the language of symbols and respond to it. A rose quartz heart can call the vibration of Chamuel, the archangel of compassionate love. A blue candle can attract Michael, the guardian and protector. A feather found on the street and placed on the altar becomes an anchor of connection with your personal angel. Nothing is random when the intention is clear. The angelic sanctuary is, in itself, a living message. It says: "Here is an open heart. Here is a soul willing to listen."

Simplicity is a virtue in this process. A space overloaded with symbols loses strength, as the mind gets distracted by excesses and loses focus on the presence. Each object should have its clear purpose. If a flower is placed, it is placed as a symbol of beauty and renewal. If a crystal is positioned, it is positioned to amplify light. Nothing is by chance, but also nothing needs to be excessively planned. Angels appreciate the spontaneity of sincere love much more than the rigidity of complex rituals.

In addition to objects, the very air of the space is prepared. Soft sounds, mantras, or angelic music can fill the environment before each connection. Sound is a powerful bridge between planes, and certain frequencies create true vibrational portals. But silence is also sacred. The consecrated space doesn't always have to be filled with sound. The true music of the sanctuary is the frequency of the heart of the one who created it.

Time also consecrates the space. A sanctuary created with love becomes, with the passing of days and practices, impregnated with light. Each prayer made there, each moment of silence or internal dialogue, leaves a vibratory trail. Angels recognize this trail. They know where they have been called and tend to return to spaces where they were welcomed with sincerity. Over time, the sanctuary becomes an anchor of light in the physical plane, a point where the vibration of your personal angel and yours intertwine in harmony.

There is a delicate reciprocity in this creation. You create the space for the angels, and the angels, in return, fill it with their light. This light, gradually, permeates not only the sanctuary but the entire surrounding environment. The whole house benefits from a point of light where the divine is welcome. Even those who do not consciously perceive it feel the lightness and peace that emanate from a consecrated space. Houses where there are angelic sanctuaries spontaneously become gentler, more harmonious, as if every corner resonates with a whisper of invisible wings.

And there is something deeper: the true sanctuary is not made of candles or crystals, but of the loving presence of the one who creates it. The external space is just a reflection of the internal space. By creating your physical altar, you are, in fact, recreating the altar of your heart. A space where your humanity and your divinity meet. Where you, small and immense at the same time, become the bridge between heaven and earth. Where your angel is no longer a distant presence, but a constant visitor and, over time, an inseparable companion.

Over time, the sanctuary ceases to be just a fixed place and begins to expand within you. Every time you sit there in silence, every time you light a candle or talk to your angel, the vibration of the space and the vibration of your soul intertwine a little more. Until the moment comes when it is no longer necessary to be physically in front of the altar to feel its presence — it begins to exist within your own chest, like a constant whisper, a delicate flame that burns even on days when life seems distant from light.

It is at this point that the separation between the sacred and the everyday dissolves. The prayer table and the dining table, the meditation corner and the reading armchair, the consecrated candle and the morning light that crosses the window — everything becomes an extension of the same internal sanctuary. Angels walk with you beyond that physical space, because they understand that the true temple was built inside, between your healed emotions, your learned silences, and your loving surrender to the invisible that accompanies you.

Creating an angelic sanctuary is an inaugural act, but never a final one. It is the first invitation, the first door opened for the angelic presence to find you and recognize you. Afterward, the sanctuary moves with you—within your voice when you pray, within your eyes when you contemplate, within your hands when they welcome. Every gesture, every choice, every conscious breath becomes part of this sacred space in motion. And the angels, those invisible companions, know that they no longer need to be called: they already dwell within you.

Chapter 6
Chakras in Channeling

Angelic channeling establishes itself as a process of conscious and integrated connection, where the subtle energy of the angelic spheres intertwines harmoniously with the energy structure of the channel itself. In this dynamic flow, the chakras assume a central role, acting as living portals, points of convergence between the physical body, emotions, thoughts, and spiritual essence. Each chakra functions as a center for receiving and translating higher frequencies, adjusting them to the channel's personal vibration and allowing communication to manifest clearly and fluidly. Unlike a simple intuitive or mediumistic technique, angelic channeling is, above all, a state of internal alignment, where each center of strength needs to be in tune for the angelic message to pass through without distortions. This alignment does not depend only on intention or faith, but on a conscious and constant relationship with one's own energy field, where each chakra is perceived as an integral and indispensable part of the process, ensuring that the flow of light travels through the being without interruptions or blockages.

Preparation for channeling, therefore, reveals itself as an act of energy self-care, in which the channel develops sensitivity to perceive the subtleties of their own field. Each chakra, from the base of the spine to the top of the head, comprises a unique vibratory sequence, adjusted both to the individuality of the one who channels and to the specific frequency of the angelic beings that approach. The root chakra, for example, anchors spiritual light in earthly experience, while the crown chakra opens to receive celestial emanation directly from the source. Between these two poles, each center of strength plays a specific role, filtering and refining energy so that it becomes understandable and applicable in practical reality. The clarity of the angelic connection depends directly on the fluidity and harmony of this internal circuit, where no chakra acts in isolation, but in constant interaction with the others. When one of these centers is blocked, the channel's perception fragments, resulting in truncated messages, confused sensations, or interpretations contaminated by fears, limiting beliefs, and unresolved emotional patterns.

By understanding that chakras are more than simple energy vortices—but true bridges between internal and external dimensions—the channel develops a deep listening to themselves, becoming capable of identifying points of tension or misalignment even before starting any channeling practice. This level of bodily and energy awareness transforms channeling into an organic experience, where the flow of angelic light is not forced or imposed, but naturally welcomed and integrated into the channel's vibratory field. The physical body, the analytical mind, emotional memory, and spiritual consciousness cease to operate as separate layers, beginning to function as a single system, where celestial light finds free passage to express itself with clarity, gentleness, and truth. In this state of internal harmony, the angelic presence is felt not as something external that comes from outside, but as an awakening of the channel's own divine essence, which recognizes itself as an active and conscious part of the great network of light that unites all dimensions of existence.

The chakras are not just isolated energy points in different parts of the body. They are portals, true vibratory bridges between your physical body, your emotions, your mind, and your soul. Each chakra is an entry and exit door for flows of information, sensations, and frequencies that cross your existence at every moment. When the chakras are misaligned, congested, or closed, your ability to perceive, interpret, and translate angelic messages is compromised. Not because the angels cannot approach, but because the channel's energy becomes like a river with stones and detours, hindering the natural flow of light.

Angelic channeling happens, essentially, through your entire energy system. It's not just "hearing with the heart," nor just an "inner vision" in the third eye. Each chakra is a sensor, each energy center participates in the reception and interpretation of the angelic presence. Therefore, preparing to channel also means taking care of the alignment and harmony of these centers of strength.

The root chakra, at the base of the spine, is the foundation of your presence in the physical world. It is what anchors you to Earth, allowing the subtle light that descends from the angelic plane to be anchored and expressed in your concrete life. A balanced root chakra ensures that channeling is not an escape from reality, but an integration between the divine and the everyday. When this chakra is blocked, there is fear, insecurity, and a feeling of disconnection from one's own life. Channeling with this chakra locked is like trying to bring water from the sky without having a container where it can be stored.

The sacral chakra, just below the navel, is the center of sensitivity and creativity. It is through it that you feel—deeply and without filters—the angelic presence as a living emotion, a pulsation of love and tenderness that crosses your body. It is also through this center that angelic energy transforms into creative inspiration, into forms, symbols, and messages that flow spontaneously when you write, draw, or speak what you receive. When the sacral chakra is blocked, there is fear of feeling, shame of one's own emotions, and difficulty in trusting the inspirations received. Channeling then becomes dry, mechanical, soulless.

The solar plexus, in the center of the abdomen, is the seat of your identity and personal power. It is what defines whether or not you trust what you receive. When this center is in harmony, you recognize your value as a channel, understand that you are worthy of receiving angelic messages, and accept with humility, but without self-annihilation, the role of bridge between worlds. When the solar plexus is weakened, the fear of inventing, the fear of not being "good enough," and the need for external validation undermine the clarity of the connection. Insecurity vibrates as interference in the channel.

The heart chakra, in the center of the chest, is the heart of the channel. It is where the angelic presence is felt for the first time, as a sweet warmth, an expansion of love without a defined origin. The heart is the direct portal between your soul and the angels, because it is the only chakra capable of instantly recognizing the vibratory signature of divine love. When the heart is closed—by fear, pain, or excessive protection—the angelic presence is still there, but you cannot feel it. It is as if the angels were gently knocking on the door of a heart that has learned to protect itself from love for fear of pain.

The throat chakra, in the throat, is the channel of expression. It is through it that the messages received take shape in the physical world, whether through speech, writing, or singing. When this chakra is blocked, there is fear of expressing what has been received, fear of making mistakes, of being judged, or of not being understood. The internal truth is trapped, and channeling loses fluidity. When the throat is aligned, words flow effortlessly, without excessive filters, with the spontaneity of someone who knows that the true value of the message is not in the perfection of the form, but in the purity of the intention.

The third eye, between the eyebrows, is the center of inner vision. It is through it that angelic images, symbols, and scenarios manifest on your mental screen. When this chakra is imbalanced, there is either an excess of disconnected images, or a complete absence of visualizations. When it is aligned, the inner vision becomes clear, fluid, and you learn to trust what you see without trying to force or control.

Finally, the crown chakra, at the top of the head, is the gateway to divine light. It is through it that the angelic presence descends as a golden or silver stream, filling your body and field. When the crown is closed, the connection seems distant, truncated, as if the angels were far away. When it is open, the feeling is of belonging, of knowing oneself to be part of something greater, of recognizing in the descending light the same light that inhabits your own being.

Channeling angels is, therefore, aligning oneself as a whole. It is not enough to open the heart and ignore the fear in the solar plexus. It is not enough to trust the third eye and forget the physical body. Each chakra is a piece of the circuit that allows angelic light to arrive, circulate, and express itself. Each center needs to be honored, heard, cared for. The purest channeling is not that of the one who climbs the highest, but that of the one who is able to open all the internal doors and allow the light to descend and ascend, freely, without barriers.

The chakras together form an energy symphony where each note matters, each pause has meaning, and each discord is reflected in the quality of the connection established. By understanding this subtle dance between the centers of strength, the channel becomes not only a receiver of messages, but an integrated being, where body, mind, soul, and spirit speak the same vibratory language. It is in this state of internal alignment that the angelic presence finds space to land, flow, and reveal itself with clarity and gentleness.

This care for one's own energy field is not just a technical preparation, but a gesture of reverence to one's own existence and to the commitment that channeling represents. By honoring each chakra, the channel recognizes that the connection with the divine is not an isolated act, restricted to the moment of practice, but a state of continuous presence, where the body is a temple, the mind is a bridge, and the soul is an open door. In this living balance, the angels do not need to shout or force passage—their light is welcomed as a natural part of the flow of life.

Channeling becomes a journey of self-discovery and deep care, where each internal adjustment reflects the intention to serve with integrity and truth. And, in this serving, the channel discovers that the light of the angels is not something external to be captured, but an ancestral spark that already burns within, waiting only for all doors to be opened to, finally, remember what has always been there.

Chapter 7
Connection Tools

Connection with angels manifests as an ancestral calling, a natural resonance between the human spirit and the celestial spheres. Before any external tool or ritual, the primordial link is established through purity of intention, openness of heart, and sincere surrender to communication that transcends words and forms. Still, throughout the ages, humanity has always felt the impulse to translate the invisible into symbols, objects, and gestures that make the sacred tangible in the physical world. This need to create bridges between planes—from matter to spirit, from the visible to the invisible—is not a weakness of the rational mind, but a legitimate expression of human essence itself, which, by nature, moves between heaven and earth. Connection tools, therefore, arise as physical extensions of an internal dialogue, delicate supports that help attune the mind, body, and soul to the subtle frequency of angelic presences. They do not directly invoke angels, as they respond to the call of the heart, but they adjust the human channel, facilitating the passage of celestial light through the vibrational field of those who open themselves to the encounter.

Within this context, each chosen tool carries a symbolic and energetic function, activating deep layers of spiritual memory and helping the channel remember its own inner language. Crystals, for example, act as guardians of planetary memory, condensing the intelligence of the Earth in their geometric structures and offering themselves as amplifiers and modulators of the personal energy of those who use them. Holding a specific crystal, placing it on the body, or integrating it into a connection space is more than a decorative gesture—it is the activation of a vibrational alliance between human consciousness and mineral essence, a fine adjustment that allows angelic light to find echo and stability in the physical field. Similarly, candles and symbols assume the role of visual and sensory guides, marking with light and form the meeting points between worlds, creating an atmosphere where the intuitive mind can quiet down and subtle perception can expand. Each lit flame, each stroke of a symbol loaded with ancestral meaning, aligns not only the physical space, but the very internal frequency of those who invite angelic presence.

The true power of connection tools, however, does not reside in their intrinsic properties, but in the conscious relationship that the channel develops with them. Instead of seeking in them an external guarantee of spiritual success, the practitioner awakens to the understanding that each crystal, each candle, each symbol is, in fact, a reflection of what already exists within themselves. The stone that resonates in the palm of the hand is the same one that reverberates in the energy centers of the body. The flame that dances on the altar is the visible expression of the internal light that burns silently in the heart. The symbol traced with devotion is the key that unlocks internal portals, allowing ancestral memories and knowledge to return to the surface of consciousness. In this sense, the tools are not shortcuts or spiritual crutches, but delicate mirrors that return to the channel the vision of their own sacredness. And, perceiving themselves as the bridge between worlds, the channel understands that the most powerful connection tool is their own conscious presence, their body that pulsates between heaven and earth, their soul that remembers, with each breath, the way home.

Crystals are one of these tools, perhaps one of the oldest and most universal. They are not just beautiful stones; they are living records of the Earth itself. Each crystal is a fragment of planetary consciousness, a silent witness to the Earth's geological and vibrational history. By holding them, by choosing them to compose an altar or an angelic connection space, we are not just decorating. We are establishing a bridge between the elements of the Earth and the celestial frequencies. Crystals are, by their nature, bridges. They condense the energy of creation in their perfect geometric forms, and this structure makes them especially receptive to subtle frequencies, such as angelic vibrations.

There is no single mandatory crystal for channeling angels. Each person resonates with different stones, and the angels who approach may indicate, through signs or inspirations, which crystals best harmonize with their presence. Clear quartz is a classic, precisely because of its ability to amplify any intention. It is a neutral receiver, willing to expand any frequency placed in it. Rose quartz, on the other hand, naturally carries the signature of love and tenderness, easily attuning to angels of emotional healing, such as Chamuel. Amethyst, with its elevated spiritual vibration, is a natural bridge to the clarity and wisdom of guardian angels and archangels.

But the function of the crystal is not to invoke the angel. Angels do not need crystals to reach us. The true function of the crystal is to adjust the channel, that is, you. By holding a crystal, by meditating with it, you tune your personal field with the stone's frequency. And this tuning creates an opening in your field that facilitates the reception of angelic presence. The crystal is like a tuning key, a small vibrational adjustment that makes your energy more receptive to the subtle light that approaches.

Candles, in turn, are another ancestral element of connection. Since time immemorial, fire has been seen as a messenger between worlds. It transforms matter—wax—into light, smoke, and heat, traversing the visible and invisible planes. Lighting a candle is not just illuminating an environment; it is lighting an intention. It is creating a focus, a luminous point that signals to angels that there, at that moment, is a soul available for the encounter.

The colors of candles can be chosen with intention or just by intuition. White candles are open doors, universal invitations to pure light. Blue candles call for the protection and strength of archangels like

Michael. Pink candles open the heart, facilitating communication with angels of love and emotional healing. Golden candles celebrate the presence of manifest divine light. But more important than color is the intention with which the candle is lit. A candle lit with reverence, with the mind and heart present, is much more powerful than a golden candle lit mechanically, without soul.

The act of lighting the candle is, in itself, a call. The simple gesture of striking the match and watching the flame rise is a silent prayer. It is as if, for an instant, the soul and matter meet at the tip of the wick, creating a bridge of light that extends beyond the visible. Angels do not need the physical flame, but they recognize the intention that created it. They approach not the candle itself, but the light that was born from your loving intention.

Symbols are the third great connection tool. And here we enter an even more intimate territory, because symbols are the direct language of the unconscious and the soul. Each symbol is a key, an energetic signature that opens specific doors within you. It is not the symbol itself that has power, but what it awakens within your field. By using a symbol in your connection space or on your body, you are signaling to the universe which door you wish to open.

The pentagram of Venus, for example, connects directly with the frequencies of divine love and cosmic beauty. The flower of life resonates with the geometric patterns of creation, adjusting your field to the universal rhythm. The eye of Horus awakens inner vision, making the mental screen more receptive to angelic images. And there are personal symbols, those that arise spontaneously in dreams or meditations, exclusive to each channel.

Angels recognize the language of symbols, because they themselves often present themselves as living symbols. An experienced channel learns to recognize their angels not only by the feeling of presence, but by small symbolic signatures—a specific color, a flower that always appears, a recurring number. These symbols are not arbitrary. They are the way the angel imprints their vibrational signature on the channel's mind. When these symbols are incorporated into physical space—drawn, sculpted, or just placed in images—they serve as anchors, facilitating reconnection with that specific presence.

Crystals, candles, and symbols are not magical elements that guarantee channeling. They are supports, physical extensions of your own desire for connection. They remind your mind and soul that this is a sacred space, a special moment. They help align your field, focus your intention, and create an atmosphere where the subtle becomes perceptible. But in the end, the true connection tool is and always will be you. Your body, your heart, your mind, and your soul are the altar, the flame, and the living symbol where angelic light finds a home.

Each tool becomes a gentle reminder that the sacred has never been distant. The crystal in your hands, the candle lit on the altar, or the symbol drawn with care are just reflections of a dialogue that has always existed, even before consciousness awakened it. They are golden threads that sew the visible to the invisible, echoing the truth that each external element is, in the end, an extension of your own being, a silent reverence to what in you is already divine.

Over time, you begin to choose your tools not by obligation or superstition, but by affinity and recognition. Each chosen crystal, each lit flame, each traced symbol reveals an aspect of your own spiritual journey—as if each object spoke an ancient language that only your soul understands. Practice ceases to be a rigid ritual and transforms into a fluid conversation, where angels are not just external presences, but luminous echoes of your own inner light awakening.

And in this constant dialogue between heaven and earth, between your hands and your heart, you learn that true connection is made of simplicity and presence. Tools are beautiful companions, but the most sacred altar is you. When the crystal rests, the candle goes out, and the symbol dissolves into memory, it is your loving intention that remains—vibrating like a discreet but constant star in the inner sky where angels always find their way back.

Chapter 8
Personal Vibration

The attunement between personal vibration and angelic frequency establishes itself as a field of mutual recognition, where each energetic pulsation emitted by the human being finds echo and response in the subtle layers of the celestial plane. Far beyond a sporadic event or an isolated mystical experience, this attunement reveals itself as a state of expanded presence, where the soul, body, and mind harmonize into a single vibrational field. In this state, communication with angels becomes a natural consequence, not something forced or artificially provoked, but a spontaneous unfolding of the very vibrational quality that the individual cultivates and emanates. The human being is, by nature, a constant emitter of frequencies, each thought, emotion, and intention reverberating in the subtle field like a note in the cosmic symphony. The ease or difficulty in perceiving angelic presence does not depend on spiritual merit or hidden privileges, but rather on the degree of attunement between personal vibration and the loving and pure frequency of these beings of light.

Personal vibration is not a fixed, immutable, or predetermined characteristic. On the contrary, it is a dynamic flow, shaped and refined at every moment by the conscious and unconscious choices the being makes. Each emotion embraced or repressed, each belief nurtured or dissolved, each thought cultivated or discarded contributes to the configuration of the vibrational field that defines a person's energetic identity. This unique vibration acts as a signature, an energetic business card that determines not only how the person is perceived by the subtle spheres, but also which frequencies they can access clearly. Angels, by their compassionate nature, do not shy away from dense vibrations or moments of human pain, but the conscious perception of their presence is only facilitated when the personal field aligns, even for brief moments, with the frequency of acceptance, tenderness, and loving openness. It is in this receptive state, where there are no internal barriers between the being and their own essence, that angelic presence becomes tangible as a warmth, an intuition, or a subtle wave of comfort and certainty.

The human heart, a vibratory center par excellence, plays a fundamental role in this process of personal tuning. More than a physical organ or a poetic symbol, the heart is a living antenna, calibrated to recognize and respond to the vibration of divine love. When this antenna is obstructed by layers of fear, self-criticism, or disconnection, the perception of angelic presence becomes diffuse, intermittent, or completely veiled. But as these layers are dissolved—not by denying pain, but by compassionately embracing each fragment of one's own history—the heart recovers its natural ability to vibrate in harmony with the angelic field. This attunement, far from demanding perfection or irreproachable purity, asks only for authenticity and presence: the courage to be whole, to recognize one's own shadows without running from them, and to allow the inner light to shine even in the most painful cracks. When the human being learns to inhabit this vibrational honesty, without masks or attempts to appear more spiritualized than they really are, the bridge with angels becomes solid and constant. They do not need to be called or invoked—they are already there, waiting only for the moment when the internal channel opens to recognize them as an inseparable part of the same flow of love and consciousness that shapes everything that exists.

Love is a word so used, so worn out by limited interpretations, that we sometimes forget what it really means in vibrational terms. For angels, love is not a passing emotion or a romantic connection between two people. Love is a frequency, a pure emanation of divine essence itself. It is the invisible thread that connects all things, from a distant star to a leaf falling in autumn. It is the invisible substance from which everything is made. When we talk about "tuning in to angels," we are, in fact, talking about learning to vibrate at this primordial frequency.

Each human being possesses a unique personal vibration, formed by layers of experiences, beliefs, emotions, and ancestral memories. This personal vibration is not static; it oscillates according to your internal state, your daily choices, and your level of consciousness. And it is precisely this personal vibration that determines how easily—or with what difficulty—you access angelic presence. Angels do not shy away from those who vibrate low, nor do they choose only those who already vibrate high. But the closer your frequency is to the frequency of love, the more natural and fluid communication between you will be.

The frequency of love is not an abstract idea. It is a real, perceptible vibration that can be felt in the body itself. It manifests as a lightness in the chest, a gentle opening in the center of the heart, a sense of belonging and security even in the face of life's uncertainties. When you are vibrating at the frequency of love, your energetic field expands, your aura shines more intensely, and angelic presence becomes almost tangible. It's as if you were speaking the same vibrational language as they do.

But the love we speak of here is not just romantic or affective love. It is essential love, the vibration that arises from the simple recognition that you are part of the same light from which the angels came. This love begins with you. Your ability to love and honor yourself is the starting point for tuning in to any being of light. This is because angels are not outside of you; they are extensions of the same source that animates your own soul. When you reject, judge, or abandon yourself, you cut off this vibrational bridge. When you learn to welcome yourself, to look at yourself with compassion, and to recognize your own light, this bridge is rebuilt—and the angels cross it.

Vibrating at the frequency of love is, therefore, an act of spiritual memory. You do not need to create this frequency from scratch. It already exists within you. What you need is to remove the blockages, fears, and layers of self-denial that stifle this vibration. Every judgment you hold against yourself or against the world is like a wall that separates you from the natural frequency of angels. Every forgiveness, every gesture of kindness, every act of care for yourself and others, is a breach in this wall. Channeling angels is learning to live without these walls.

That's why preparation for channeling is not just technical, but emotional and vibrational. It is not enough to learn the steps, know the names, or memorize prayers. It is necessary to feel. It is necessary to remember what it is like to live open, without rigid defenses, without armors of fear or cynicism. This openness is not naive vulnerability; it is spiritual courage. It is knowing that your true protection does not come from closing off, but from connecting with this loving frequency that sustains and permeates everything.

And here is an essential paradox: the more you seek angelic connection with effort and anxiety, the more distant it seems. Because excessive effort usually arises from the belief that you are separate, that you need to "reach" the angels as if they were somewhere far from you. But the truth is that they are as close as your own breath. They do not need to be "sought." They just need to be recognized—and this recognition happens when you relax and allow the love, already present, to fill your field.

This relaxation, however, does not mean passivity. It means active trust. It means taking care of your personal vibration like someone taking care of a garden. Each thought, each word, each choice is a seed planted in this vibrational garden. When you choose thoughts of fear, unworthiness, or separation, you sow thorns in this field. When you choose thoughts of kindness, gratitude, and openness, you sow flowers. Angels walk more easily in flowery gardens.

It is important to remember that vibrating at the frequency of love does not mean always being happy or "positive." This is a distortion. True love includes welcoming pain, shadow, and difficult emotions with compassion, without judgment. It is possible to vibrate in love even on days when you cry or feel fear. Because love is not the absence of pain, but the conscious and compassionate presence before it. Angels do not turn away when you suffer. They come even closer, precisely because sincere suffering is an open door to divine care. What hinders connection is not the pain itself, but rigidity and refusal to feel it.

As you learn to keep your personal vibration aligned with love, channeling ceases to be an isolated event and becomes a natural state of being. You become a permanent channel, even when you are not sitting in meditation or holding a crystal. Angels begin to inhabit your daily life, your small choices, your simple gestures. And you realize that channeling is not bringing something from the outside in, but allowing something that is already inside you to express itself freely.

True angelic connection reveals itself not as a distant technique, but as a reunion with your own essential nature. Each adjustment in your personal vibration is a silent invitation to the angels, a subtle gesture of mutual recognition between your soul and the light they emanate. When you walk through the world with this living memory—that your frequency is an extension of their frequency—the veil between the planes thins, and angelic presence ceases to be an extraordinary event and becomes a daily, subtle, and loving companionship.

Understanding your personal vibration is, fundamentally, remembering that you are a conscious link between earth and heaven. Each emotion welcomed, each thought softened, each word spoken with love adjusts your field like someone tuning an instrument to play along with the invisible choir of angels. This tuning does not require perfection, but presence. It does not ask for untouchable purity, but vibrational honesty—the courage to be whole, to allow yourself to feel and overflow, knowing that it is precisely in the acceptance of what is that love reveals itself.

It is in this inner space of acceptance and truth that angels approach most clearly. Not because they choose where to be, but because it is in this state of openness and sincerity that you are finally able to perceive them. Your personal vibration is the key and the door, the call and the answer. And when that door opens, there is no separation between you and them — only the continuous flow of the same light, flowing inside and out, like a river that never stopped running.

Chapter 9
Prayers and Invocations

Prayers and invocations constitute a subtle and powerful movement of alignment between the human essence and the angelic presence. More than simple words spoken to the wind or automatic repetitions of memorized texts, they are vibrational expressions that, when pronounced with intention and truth, adjust the frequency of one's being to the luminous field of the angels. Each word carries within it a specific vibration, a sonic pulse that crosses the boundaries of the physical and resonates in the subtle layers of existence. When a prayer is born from authenticity, it not only pierces the veil between worlds but also reveals to the channel itself its innate capacity to be a bridge between the visible and the invisible. The conscious word is a creative act, a spark of light that organizes the internal and external space, allowing the vibrational field to become receptive to the angelic presence that already awaits, ever near, merely waiting for this door to open.

More than direct communication with angels, prayer is a gesture of remembrance and recognition. By invoking a presence, whether through a sacred name, a spontaneous phrase, or an ancestral call, the channel is not just directing their intention outward but reactivating within themselves the frequency corresponding to that being of light. Each angel carries in their vibrational signature a specific quality — protection, healing, guidance, love, or clarity — and by pronouncing the name of that angel or invoking them with an open heart, the channel activates within themselves that very quality. Invoking Michael is awakening one's own spiritual courage; calling upon Raphael is recognizing the internal healer who dwells in every cell of the body and every layer of the soul. This understanding transforms prayer from an external request to a journey of internal reconnection, where each word becomes a key to accessing what the channel itself has always been: an extension of the divine light that angels personify.

The true power of invocations does not reside in their form or antiquity, but in the vibrational truth with which they are uttered. A spontaneous prayer, born of vulnerability and the sincerity of a moment of surrender, resonates more strongly in the angelic spheres than the most elaborate invocation repeated without inner connection. This is because angels do not respond to the aesthetics of words, but to the frequency that sustains them. When the word is shaped by love, faith, and full presence, it transforms into a sonic portal, a vibrational bridge between planes. But for this portal to open, it is necessary that the prayer be born not only from the mind but from the heart. The heart is the vibrational center capable of recognizing the angelic signature clearly, and when words emerge from this sacred inner space, they carry with them the essential truth that angels recognize instantly: the pure vibration of the soul seeking communion with its own source.

Prayers and invocations, therefore, are not just spiritual techniques or external tools to attract celestial presences. They are, above all, instruments of personal realignment, moments when the channel abandons the distractions of the ego and the superficial mind and delves into the sacred space of feeling. In this dive, the veil between worlds becomes diaphanous, and the angelic presence, which was never distant, reveals itself as a loving extension of the praying being itself. Understanding that prayer is not a call to bring something external but an invitation to remember what already dwells in one's heart, the channel discovers that words are merely sonic maps pointing to the true temple: the loving silence where angels and souls have danced together since the beginning of time.

The word, when pronounced with intention and consciousness, is a creative act. The universe was shaped by primordial vibrations, and each word carries a fraction of this creative force. When you pray, invoke, or pronounce the name of an angel, you are not merely transmitting a desire. You are shaping the energetic space around you. You are signaling to the invisible spheres which frequency you wish to attract. The word is sound, and sound is vibration. In essence, speaking with angels is learning to vibrate along with them.

But it's not about memorizing sacred words or repeating ancient formulas just because they were written in spiritual books. The most powerful prayer is the one that is born from your own heart. The prayer you create, with your simple and sincere words, carries a unique vibrational signature: yours. And angels recognize this signature. They do not respond to the beauty of form, but to the truth of intention. A simple prayer, spoken with sincerity, resonates in the heavens more strongly than a complex invocation pronounced without soul.

Still, there is wisdom in tradition. Words and phrases that have been used for centuries to invoke the angelic presence carry a vibrational trail. Every time someone, in any time or place, invoked an angel with sincere faith, that vibration was recorded in the fabric of the universe. When you use those words today, you are connecting to that accumulated current of devotion. You are joining an egregore of faith that strengthens your own intention.

But words are just the beginning. True prayer is an internal movement. It begins in the mind, takes shape on the lips, but needs to bloom in the heart for it to truly cross the planes. Praying mechanically is like knocking on a door without waiting for an answer. Invoking an angel with an open heart is like opening the door yourself and inviting the presence to enter. The sound of prayer is important, but the internal silence that accompanies it is essential. It is in this silence that the answer arrives.

Many believe that invoking angels requires elaborate rituals, precise gestures, or ancient words in unknown languages. This is a myth. Angels do not speak a specific language; they speak the language of the soul. They understand your words not by the language itself, but by the vibration they emit. The phrase "I am ready to listen" can be as powerful as a long ancestral prayer, if said with truth.

However, there is a special beauty in invoking an angel by name. The name is a vibrational signature. Each angelic name carries within it the echo of the function, essence, and mission of that angel. When you pronounce the name of Michael, Raphael, Chamuel, or any other, you are not just calling a distant entity. You are adjusting your own field to tune in to the specific frequency of that being. It's like adjusting the dial of a radio station. The name is the frequency. The intention is the signal. And faith is the antenna.

This is the true function of invocations. They do not force angels to come to you. Angels do not respond to order; they respond to attunement. To invoke is to tune in. When you call upon an angel, the call resonates within you before echoing outward. You are not just asking for an external presence. You are awakening, within your own being, the part of you that is already attuned to that angelic presence. Invoking Michael is awakening your own courage. Invoking Raphael is activating your own healing power. Invoking Chamuel is remembering your own capacity to love.

This is a secret forgotten by many: true invocation is not just an outward request, but an inward remembrance. It is an invitation for the light that angels represent to find an echo in the light you already carry. Angels do not descend from heaven because you called them. They emerge from your own field because you have opened yourself to recognize them.

The words of a prayer or invocation, therefore, are like the melody of a divine song. Each word is a note. But it is not enough to play the right notes. You must feel the music. And that music is love. Without love, words are just empty sounds. With love, each word becomes a key of light.

There are times when no words are necessary. The silent soul invokes angels with a simple sigh, a look to the sky, a sincere tear. Angels hear these silent prayers with the same clarity with which they hear words shouted to the wind. Sound is not essential to them, but it is to you. When you pronounce a prayer aloud, you anchor your intention in the physical world. You give sonic form to your inner will. And this, to your own mind and heart, is an act of confirmation and presence.

Creating your own prayers is an exercise in trust. In the beginning, the mind questions. Am I saying it right? Do angels hear me? But over time, you realize that there is no right or wrong. There is only truth or emptiness. Every true prayer is heard. Every sincere invocation is answered. Perhaps not in the way you expect, but always in the way your soul needs.

Prayer is a bridge between worlds, but also between parts of yourself. It connects your mind to your heart, your intention to your soul, your desire to the divine presence. It transforms an ordinary moment into a sacred space. It turns a silent room into a temple. It transforms a whisper into a celestial trumpet. Because when you pray, you are not just calling the angels. You are reminding yourself that they have always been here.

And so, each whispered or silently thought prayer becomes a trail of light, an invisible path where your soul walks to meet the angelic presence. There is no real distance between the human and the divine — only layers of forgetfulness and distraction that the conscious word has the power to dissipate. When you invoke, it is not the angel who needs to find the way to you; it is you who, through the vibration of prayer, rediscovers the clarity of who you have always been: a soul capable of conversing with heaven.

Over time, you discover that the deepest prayers are not those memorized or recited as a duty, but those that are born from the present moment, from the raw and luminous truth of your own feeling. The prayer of weariness, the invocation of fear, the plea of hope, and spontaneous gratitude — all of them open doors. Angels do not move by perfect sound, but by the vibrant honesty that echoes from each sincere word. They recognize your call because the love you seek is the same that composes them.

Prayers and invocations become a living art, a continuous conversation where the separation between human and celestial dissolves. With each word that is born, you adjust your own field, tune your frequency, and recall, little by little, that the voice that calls and the light that answers are, at their core, one and the same— echoing in the sacred silence where angels and souls have danced together since the beginning of time.

Chapter 10
Feeling the Angelic Presence

The experience of the first contact with the angelic presence is not translated by spectacular images or thunderous external manifestations; it is revealed in subtle layers, permeated by a silent intimacy between the visible and the invisible. Even before the conscious mind perceives it, the body and soul already recognize this ancestral presence, for the connection with angels precedes the very linear memory of this existence. The encounter with these luminous presences does not depend on dogmas or established beliefs, as their essence transcends any specific form. It manifests as an inner call, a memory engraved in the innermost fibers of being, awakened in moments of spontaneous openness when the soul sighs for something greater than the material world can offer. The approach of an angel is not an invasion, but a reunion that resonates in the invisible layers of being, where the spirit has never separated from the primordial source. There is a mutual recognition, a subtle vibratory exchange, where the angel offers its compassionate presence and the human being, even without understanding, responds with an instinctive vulnerability, allowing itself to be touched by a light that is, at the same time, familiar and ineffable.

This first approach rarely obeys the expectations of the rational mind, accustomed to framing spiritual experiences in predictable or dramatized scenarios. Angels move in the texture of the sensitive, where the body and the heart become the first instruments of perception. The skin captures subtle variations in temperature, shivers that spring up without apparent physical cause, as if a breeze from another dimension crossed the limits of matter. The heart, in turn, responds with an involuntary opening, a dilation that welcomes the loving vibration without needing to name it or understand it. This love that arrives without demanding, without asking for explanations or merits, carries the unmistakable signature of the angelic presence. It is not a conditioned love or directed at something or someone; it is a state of being, a vibratory field where the ego dissolves and the being recognizes itself as part of a loving and compassionate whole. This love, which touches the heart without asking permission, is the first foundation on which the bond with angels is built, a bond that does not need to be rationalized to be real.

The mind, naturally distrustful of what escapes its control parameters, tends to resist subtle contact. It seeks tangible evidence, concrete signs that can be recorded, cataloged, and compared with external references. However, the language of angels does not fit into the rigid molds of the analytical mind. It speaks directly to feeling, to the inner silence where the deepest layers of being keep alive the memory of the divine. The first contact with the angelic presence is, in essence, an invitation to transcend the need for proof and immerse oneself in sensory trust, where truth does not need to be validated to be felt. This trust, when cultivated with surrender and internal listening, allows the angelic presence to become part of the internal landscape of the soul, not as an isolated or extraordinary event, but as a continuous flow of silent connection. The first contact, therefore, is not the beginning of something external, but the revelation of a relationship that has always existed — an invisible thread that links the human heart to the heart of creation, pulsing gently in the rhythm of unconditional love.

For many, this first contact happens even before a conscious search exists. It is that inexplicable presence felt in childhood, when something invisible seemed to calm a nocturnal fear or accompany solitary games. It is that invisible hand that held your chest in the moment of greatest pain and transformed absolute despair into a strange peace. Angels rarely invade. They arrive gently, waiting for the moment when your soul is ready to recognize them, even if the mind does not yet understand.

When the conscious call arises and you decide, with clear intention, to open yourself to contact, it is natural for the mind to expect something grand. We want to see, hear, know with absolute clarity that the contact is real. But angels do not live in human logic. They do not respond to the ego's expectation. They reveal themselves in the measure of your openness, and openness is not a demand; it is a surrender. The first contact is rarely a concrete manifestation. It is, almost always, a subtle change in the air around you. A lightness in the environment, a temperature change that has no explanation, a shiver that runs through the skin for no apparent reason.

The body feels first. Before the mind captures any word or image, the body registers the approach of angelic light. The breath changes — it deepens or is suspended for an instant. The skin feels something similar to an internal breeze. Sometimes, it is a gentle warmth that envelops the hands or chest. Other times, it is like a veil of freshness passing over the face. The body knows. It recognizes the presence even before you understand. Because, in essence, your physical body is an extension of the Earth — and the Earth has recognized angels from the beginning.

After the body, the heart responds. Not as a common emotion, but as an expansion. The chest widens, as if the internal space increased to accommodate something greater than you. It is a feeling of tenderness without cause. A love that needs no motive or recipient. It is just there. Pure, present, complete. This is the most common vibratory signature of angels: unconditional love, which fills and envelops without demanding anything in return. When you feel this, even for an instant, you are in contact.

The mind, however, has difficulty accepting something so subtle. It wants proof, explanations, external confirmations. And this is where many break off the first contact even before understanding it. The mind doubts, analyzes, compares with unrealistic expectations created by movies or books. And, in this search for a spectacular manifestation, it fails to perceive the silent miracle that is already happening. The true first contact is not the explosion of light, but the subtle presence that settles and changes something inside you forever.

Angels know you need time to recognize this presence. Therefore, they rarely impose themselves. They arrive, offer their vibration, and wait. If you recoil, close yourself, or deny, they do not argue. They just recoil too, waiting for a new opening. But if you allow yourself to feel, without forcing, without trying to fit the experience into ready-made molds, something profound happens. Trust awakens. Not the trust in the experience itself, but the trust in your own feeling. You begin to realize that what seemed like "imagination" is, in fact, a real conversation — only in another language.

This language is feeling. The first contact is, first and foremost, a dance between the angel's subtle presence and your willingness to feel without controlling. Each person feels in a different way. For some, the first contact is visual — flashes of light, colors appearing in closed eyes. For others, it is auditory — a sweet buzzing in the ears, like distant bells or the beating of wings. But, for most, it is simply an inner certainty, as if a dormant memory were awakened. You don't know how you know — but you know.

And that is how angels present themselves: not as something external that invades, but as something internal that is recognized. The angel who comes to meet you is not a stranger. It is a presence that your soul already knows. Someone who has been with you before this life, before this body. Someone who knows your silences and your unspoken prayers. Therefore, the first contact is, in essence, a reunion. A return home.

The physical space where this contact happens matters little to angels, but it matters to you. Creating a peaceful environment, lighting a candle, or holding a crystal is not a spiritual requirement — it is a gesture of self-care. It is preparing your own heart for the subtle. And the subtle needs space. It needs silence. Not absolute silence of the external environment, but inner silence — that instant when the voices of the mind stop demanding and the heart just listens.

When the first contact happens, something changes forever. Even if you try to rationalize, explain, or deny, something inside you already knows. Even if you never feel the same presence in the same way again, the door has been opened. And once opened, it never closes completely. Because it is not a door between you and the angel. It is a door between you and yourself — between the part of you that lives in matter and the part that never left the light.

After the first contact, internal tests come. The mind doubts, the ego questions. Was it real? Was it my imagination? Did I make it up? These questions are natural. They are not a sign of failure, but a sign that you are crossing the border between the visible and the invisible. Doubt is part of the journey, but it does not define the truth. The truth is what remained inside you, even after the moment passed. The love you felt cannot be made up. The peace that went through your body cannot be fabricated. And even if the mind doubts, the heart remembers.

And it is this silent remembering that sustains the entire journey. Because the first contact with the angelic presence is not just a spiritual event — it is a seed planted in the soil of the soul, capable of germinating even under the storms of doubt and forgetfulness. The mind may deny, the ego may distrust, but the body and the heart keep the living memory of that instant when subtle light touched matter. That touch, however brief, is the reminder that you were never really alone.

With time, you discover that angelic presence isn't something that comes and goes, but something that pulses like an invisible thread connecting your essence to the origin of everything. It doesn't depend on grand revelations or spectacular signs, because it's in the calm breath in the face of fear, in the inexplicable confidence that sprouts in the midst of chaos, in the invisible embrace that envelops when words fail. Every time you quiet down and feel, without forcing, this presence rekindles — not because it has moved away, but because you remembered to feel. The first contact turns into a living relationship, a dialogue that crosses ordinary days and silent nights. You learn that you don't need to chase after angelic presence, because it already walks by your side. You don't need to prove anything, nor strive to be worthy of feeling it. Just make space, open your heart and trust that, whenever you remember to look inside, it will be there — as subtle as a breath, as constant as the light that never stopped shining in you.

Chapter 11
Clearing Energy Blocks

Angelical energy permeates space with a loving subtlety and a vibration that surpasses the limits of common perception, flowing without resistance whenever it finds a heart willing to receive it. This luminous frequency, which carries within it the purity of the divine source, does not need to forcefully break through barriers or break internal structures to make itself present. It merely responds to the natural openness of each being, expanding to the exact extent of the receptivity offered. The true obstacle to this reception lies not in the intensity or absence of the angelic presence, but in the layers of protection that the human being has built along their journey. These layers, constituted by dense memories, crystallized beliefs, and pains that have been carefully guarded to avoid new suffering, end up acting as filters that limit the perception and the free flow of divine light. They are not spiritual flaws or any deficiency in the soul; they are merely reflections of the emotional survival strategies that the spirit adopts when going through experiences of disconnection, loss, or rejection. These layers, invisible to the physical eyes, become vibrational records in the energy field, influencing how each person feels, perceives, and relates to the subtle frequencies around them, including the angelic presence.

The construction of these barriers is, in its essence, a natural mechanism of the psyche and the spirit in the face of a world that frequently denies or distorts the essential truth of being. From the first years of life, we learn to condition love to approval, to suffocate our most legitimate emotions to be accepted, and to mold ourselves to external expectations, even if it means disconnecting essential parts of who we truly are. Every time an intense emotion is repressed, an authentic desire is denied, or a deep pain is silenced, a fragment of our original light is hidden under layers of protection. These layers, although created with the intention of preserving emotional integrity, end up forming true blockages in the natural flow of vital energy and in the ability to perceive the angelic presence clearly and directly. This occurs because the same openness necessary to fully feel life is the one that allows the entry of subtle light. When this openness is compromised, spiritual perception also becomes diffuse, like a message received through a dense fog.

Clearing energy blocks is not just an isolated spiritual practice, but a continuous act of reconnecting with one's own essence and rescuing the original trust that we are worthy of receiving and sustaining divine light. This process does not seek to eliminate or erase the pains and stories that have shaped us, but rather to integrate them with love and awareness, dissolving the rigid layers that have formed around them. The angelic presence, unlike an invasive external force, is a loving manifestation that patiently awaits each permission granted by the heart. It approaches with respect, awaiting the moment when the being feels ready to release each layer of pain and fear, replacing them with trust and self-love. Clearing blocks, therefore, is a journey of returning to the center, where the angelic presence and the essential truth of the human being meet, recognizing themselves as complementary expressions of the same luminous source, eternally connected, even when the layers of protection create the illusion of separation.

These blocks are not spiritual defects or character flaws. They are part of the human condition. We all carry scars, painful learnings, and emotional inheritances that have shaped us. Each experience of rejection, each moment when we felt unworthy of love, each time we suffocated a legitimate emotion to be accepted, all of this accumulates in the energy field. Not as a punishment, but as layers of protection that the mind creates to try to avoid new pains. These layers, over time, become so dense that they block not only the natural flow of vital energy, but also the perception of the angelic presence.

The angels do not move away because of these blocks. They do not judge your scars. They see them as what they truly are: attempts by your soul to survive in a world often harsh and disconnected from the source. However, they also know that, while these blocks are present, communication between you will be filtered, distorted, or fragmented. Not because they cannot speak to you, but because your field cannot receive clearly.

Clearing these blocks is, therefore, an act of self-love and spiritual openness. It is not a task that is done once and resolved. It is a continuous process, a journey of undoing the layers of fear and rediscovering the original trust that you are worthy of light, worthy of love, and worthy of the angelic presence. Each layer removed not only facilitates channeling but returns to you parts of yourself that were trapped in old pains. It is a process of liberation, where the opening to the angels and the opening to your own essence walk together.

Energy blocks can manifest in many ways. Some appear as a feeling of heaviness in the body, as if something invisible were pulling you down whenever you try to connect. Others arise as internal voices that question and sabotage — "This is just in my head," "I'm not spiritual enough," "Who am I to talk to angels?" These voices are not yours. They are echoes of collective memories, inherited beliefs, and past experiences where love was denied or conditioned. Recognizing them is the first step to dissolving them.

There are also deep emotional blocks — those pains that were buried because, at the time they happened, they were too great to be processed. Traumas, abandonments, losses. Each of these wounds creates a contraction in the energy field. And this contraction becomes a blind spot, an area where light cannot fully enter. Not because the angels do not wish to heal this pain, but because you yourself, often without realizing it, keep this area closed, believing that reopening contact with it would bring unbearable pain.

The truth is that angelic light never forces entry. It respects every layer of protection you have created. But, at the same time, it remains there, soft and constant, waiting for your consent. Clearing blocks is not a violent act. It is a loving permission for light to enter, not to tear down your defenses, but to dissolve them gently, to the extent that you are ready. The angels never invade. They wait for your yes. And that yes can be as simple as a sincere prayer: "I am ready to release what no longer serves me."

Some blocks dissolve smoothly, like ice melting in the sun. Others need to be seen, felt, and embraced before transforming. Each block holds a story, and that story deserves to be heard. Therefore, clearing is not just energetic — it is also emotional. By opening yourself to the angels, you open yourself to your own truth, to those parts of you that were frozen in time, waiting to be rescued. Clearing a block is rescuing a part of you that was trapped in pain. And this rescue is only possible through love and compassion for yourself.

The angels do not come to replace you in this process. They come to support. They hold your hands as you look at your shadows. They envelop you with invisible wings when the old pain resurfaces. They whisper the truth you have forgotten: you are loved, even with your scars. You are worthy of light, even with your doubts. You are deserving of the angelic presence, not because you are perfect, but because you are human.

And it is precisely this humanity — this mixture of light and shadow, of fear and courage — that makes you a perfect channel. It is not the absence of blocks that makes someone a good channeler. It is the willingness to look at them with love and not with judgment. Each block dissolved not only clears the channel but expands your capacity for compassion. Because, by releasing your own pains, you become able to embrace the pain of the world without closing your heart.

Clearing blocks is, therefore, an inseparable part of preparing for angelic channeling. Not because the angels demand perfection, but because your soul deserves this lightness. And as each layer of fear dissolves, each belief of unworthiness is undone, and each old pain is embraced and released, something magical happens: you realize that the angels have never been far away. They have always been on the other side of these layers, waiting for you to remember that you have never been separated from the light.

As each layer is dissolved and each internal space is bathed in this subtle and loving light, the perception of the sacred within you expands. It is not just about feeling the angelic presence around, but about recognizing that this same presence dwells in your own being. The angels do not come from outside, as distant visitors. They awaken from within, like echoes of a truth that has always been there — you are part of the same luminous source that they emanate. Clearing blocks is, ultimately, remembering your own divine nature, which never ceased to exist, merely became buried under layers of fear and forgetfulness.

And in this remembrance, each encounter with a block ceases to be a battle and transforms into a conversation. The old pain, once feared, becomes welcomed like a frightened child who just needs to be heard. Judgment dissolves, giving way to a loving curiosity about your own stories, your own abysses. The angels do not come to correct who you are, but to walk alongside you as you explore every hidden corner of your soul, with the certainty that even the darkest parts deserve love and light.

Over time, this journey of clearing and rescuing ceases to be an effort and becomes a natural practice, almost a dance between the angelic light and the light of your essence. With each layer released, a new internal space opens for the sacred to manifest. And, in the silence of this clean and welcoming space, the dialogue with the angels becomes clear, fluid, as if the soul and the celestial presence were just two faces of the same love, finally meeting again, without barriers, without fear, only in communion.

Chapter 12
Expanded Sensitivity

Expanded sensitivity emerges as a natural unfolding of human consciousness opening beyond conventional senses, allowing perception to extend smoothly to the subtler layers of reality. It's not about acquiring a new skill or developing something external to who you already are, but about accessing an innate capacity, long present in your being, though often muffled by cultural conditioning and emotional defenses built throughout life. From the first years of existence, the mind learns to privilege the visible and tangible, relegating the subtle sensory to a secondary plane, labeling it as fantasy, coincidence, or reverie. However, the soul never loses its ability to feel the invisible fabric that sustains existence. The call to expanded sensitivity is, therefore, a reconnection with this deep listening, where every vibration, every whisper, and every presence becomes accessible not through concentrated effort, but through the willingness to feel, welcome, and trust.

This expansion of perception is, first and foremost, a return to the completeness of being, where mind, body, and spirit work in harmony to decode the messages that come from the subtle planes. The body, often underestimated in this process, functions as a living antenna, capturing sensations, shivers, subtle pressures, and temperature changes that signal encounters with angelic frequencies. The intuitive mind, free from the need to control or explain, learns to allow images, words, and knowledge to sprout spontaneously, without demanding immediate proof or justifications. And the spirit, always connected to its divine origin, recognizes the vibrational signature of each loving presence that approaches, distinguishing it with the clarity of someone recognizing an old friend. This broad and fluid attunement is the core of expanded sensitivity: the ability to perceive the sacred in the intervals, in the silences, in the subtle details that the conditioned mind has learned to ignore.

Expanded sensitivity, therefore, is not a gift granted to a few or a skill restricted to mystics and mediums. It is a natural memory of the soul, accessible to any human being willing to unlearn the rigid filters that stifle intuitive perception. Unlearning to doubt the first sensory impulse. Unlearning to disqualify perceptions that do not fit into logical explanations. Unlearning to mistrust one's own inner wisdom. This sensitivity is not a portal to get lost in parallel worlds or escape the present reality; on the contrary, it is an amplification of presence in the here and now. The more expanded, the more conscious and grounded the person becomes, able to feel the subtle flow of life in every encounter, in every environment, in every daily decision. And in this amplification, communication with angels ceases to be an isolated or extraordinary event and becomes an organic part of the very way of existing, where the line between the visible and the invisible dissolves, revealing that both have always been faces of the same sacred reality.

This expanded sensitivity is not a gift restricted to mediums or born seers. It is a natural capacity of every human being. Everyone, without exception, has the potential to see, hear, and feel the subtle — because everyone, without exception, is part of the subtle. What happens, in most cases, is that the mind learns from an early age to mistrust what cannot be explained. The child who sees a light dancing in the room or hears a sweet whisper in the silence of the night is soon taught to ignore these perceptions as fantasy or illusion. Over time, this learning becomes second nature, and the original sensitivity retracts, like a flower that closes to protect its petals.

But this flower never dies. Sensitivity, even muffled, remains alive. And the call to angelic channeling is often the first breath of fresh air that encourages this flower to reopen. Expanded sensitivity is this ability to perceive what exists beyond the common visible and audible. It is a broadened sense, which includes the physical body but goes far beyond it. And each person has a preferred door to this expansion.

Some see. This is clairvoyance — the ability to see images, symbols, or even angelic forms with the inner eyes, or even with the physical eyes. This vision is rarely a clear vision, like looking at a person in front of you. It is, most of the time, a subtle vision that happens within the mind, like images that arise spontaneously, without effort. In the beginning, clairvoyance mixes with imagination. And this is natural, because imagination is the screen where the subtle projects itself. The challenge is to learn to trust the image that arises without needing the validation of the logical mind. Not all clairvoyance is cinematic. Often, it is just a quick visual impression — a flash, a contour, a color that appears and disappears. But this brief image can carry entire volumes of information.

Others hear. This is clairaudience — the ability to capture sounds, words, or melodies coming from the subtle plane. Like vision, this hearing is rarely external. It's like an inner voice, but it sounds different from the voice of your own thoughts. It is a voice with texture, with tone, with a tenderness or firmness that is not yours. This voice can arrive as clear words or as symbolic sounds — soft bells, incomplete whispers, or even rhythmic beats. Some hear entire melodies, as if each angel had its own song. In the beginning, this hearing mixes with common thoughts, and the channel doubts whether they are hearing something real or just talking to themselves. But, with time and practice, clairaudience gains its own contour. The angel's voice is recognized not by the content, but by the peace or clarity it leaves behind.

And there are those who feel. This is claircognizance — the direct perception of truth, without visual or auditory intermediaries. It is a knowledge that springs whole, as if the information were already there all the time, just waiting for the mind to quiet down to recognize it. Claircognizance is the subtlest gift and, therefore, one of the most challenging to trust. Because there is no external proof, no image to describe, no sound to repeat. There is only a certainty, which settles in the body and soul as something obvious. "I know." Without knowing how. Without explanation. Just clarity, solid as a rock and soft as a breath. Angels love to communicate this way, because it is the closest form of direct communication between souls. There is no noise. There is no interpretation. There is only truth.

These three doors — seeing, hearing, and feeling — are not exclusive. Most people have a predominant door, but with time and practice, they can all open. Those who start by seeing can, over time, start hearing. Those who start by hearing can, one day, feel before even hearing. And those who only feel, over time, can start to see or hear. Because expanded sensitivity is, in essence, a total opening of being. It's not about choosing a way to perceive, but about being whole, available to receive the light in whatever way it wants to arrive.

Angels do not choose a single door to enter. They adjust to the channel. If your heart is more open than your mind, they speak through feeling. If you have a naturally visual mind, they project images. If your connection with sound is deep, they approach as voice or melody. And even if you think, in the beginning, that you have no gift at all, that is not true. Expanded sensitivity is not a gift granted to a few. It is a dormant capacity in everyone.

Awakening this sensitivity is often a process of unlearning. Unlearning to doubt what you feel. Unlearning to demand proof all the time. Unlearning to measure every perception with the ruler of logic. The subtle cannot be weighed, measured, or fit into linear explanations. It can only be felt, accepted, and trusted.

And there is something even deeper: expanded sensitivity is not just a tool for channeling angels. It is an expansion of your own consciousness. It allows you to perceive not only angels but all of life in another way. You feel the vibration of people, words, places. You become more aware of how each choice affects your field. You learn to recognize when an emotion is yours and when it is just a passing cloud coming from the environment.

Over time, this expanded sensitivity ceases to be a sporadic experience or reserved for moments of spiritual connection and begins to permeate every aspect of life. It's as if a new pair of inner eyes opened, allowing you to see the reality behind appearances, the invisible thread that unites every encounter, every sensation, every silence. You become a constant receiver, not because you are looking for messages all the time, but because you learn to inhabit the present with such full presence that the subtle no longer needs to shout to be heard. It reveals itself in the simple, in the everyday, in the instant that previously went unnoticed.

And this expansion of perception does not mean carrying the weight of the world, but developing a kind of sensitive intelligence, a wisdom that knows how to differentiate what is yours and what is another's, what is truth and what is an echo of old illusions. Angels do not want you to become a fragile antenna, at the mercy of every vibration around you, but a grounded channel, who knows how to filter, choose, welcome, and, when necessary, protect yourself. True sensitivity is not vulnerability without boundaries — it is openness with discernment, it is listening with the heart without abandoning the center.

This is the true invitation of expanded sensitivity: to allow your consciousness to grow beyond the analytical mind, but without denying lucidity; to expand your feeling without getting lost in it; to open yourself to the invisible without disconnecting from the ground. Because angelic channeling is not a call to escape reality, but to inhabit it more fully, more awake, and more truly. Angels do not speak of a distant heaven. They speak of the sacred earth you tread now — and teach that it is exactly here, with feet firmly on the world, that the subtle and the divine can reveal themselves.

Chapter 13
Personal Angels and Universal Angels

Within the vast field of connection with the angelic realms, a subtle and essential dynamic emerges, differentiating the angels who walk hand in hand with your soul throughout all your existences from those who approach as cosmic forces of support in specific moments. Even before any direct communication is established, it is this loving presence that shapes the foundation of your spiritual journey, silently intertwining with your energy field and your soul's purpose. These angels, often called personal angels, do not arise from an arbitrary designation, nor from a random choice made at some point in your current incarnation. They are vibrational extensions of your own being, guardians of your purest essence, ancestral companions whose existence is directly linked to your evolution. They not only witness your choices, your falls, and your ascensions over time, but also guard the invisible threads that connect your different lives into a single fabric of learning and expansion. It is with them that your heart converses even when your mind silences, and it is from them that the soft and familiar voice that has rescued you countless times from the abyss of doubt or hopelessness springs.

The presence of these personal angels does not depend on merit, nor on any kind of spiritual achievement. They do not arrive as a prize or as recognition of an achieved evolution. They simply are, always, because the connection between your soul and theirs predates any earthly experience. It is as if they were guardians of your original map, keeping alive the vibrational memory of who you really are, even when your circumstances make you forget. This bond, woven in layers of unconditional love, makes communication with these angels particularly intimate and natural. They know your shadows, your resistances, your karmic repetitions, and your hidden pains—and yet, or precisely because of this, they remain by your side without judgment, only with the loving firmness of those who know that each fall is just part of the way back home. By recognizing this constant presence, you begin to realize that your relationship with your personal angel is not based on invocation or formality, but on trust and surrender. He does not need to be called, because he already inhabits the silent spaces between your thoughts and your deepest emotions.

But beyond this intimate and ancestral presence, there are also the greater forces—the universal angels—whose action transcends the individuality of a specific soul and extends like a river of light serving humanity as a whole. These angels do not belong to anyone in particular, but respond to the collective vibration of sincere prayer, shared despair, or the pure intention of healing and transformation. They are divine intelligences that carry within them specific frequencies from the Source, expressing archetypal qualities such as protection, wisdom, healing, compassion, and courage. Each of them is a direct emanation of these cosmic virtues, acting not only to support individuals, but to balance planetary flows, dissolve collective energetic accumulations, and sustain large-scale awakening processes. They do not come to fill emotional gaps or to rescue a specific soul, but to anchor a divine quality in the vibrational fabric of Earth, serving any human being whose vibration resonates with that frequency at a given moment.

The interaction between personal angels and universal angels is, therefore, a harmonious dance between the intimate and the cosmic, the singular and the collective. The personal angel sustains the unique flame of your essence, accompanying you in the processes of self-knowledge and personal integration. He speaks the language of your soul, adapting each message to your history and your specific sensitivity. Universal angels speak an archetypal language, whose words do not belong to you, but echo through you as waves of a greater wisdom that surpasses your individual existence. When you open yourself to channel these universal presences, you are not only receiving guidance for your own journey, but becoming an anchor point for that divine frequency to reach Earth, benefiting other beings beyond yourself. This intertwining of presences—one that walks within your heart and another that spills over your soul like cosmic rain—creates the unique tapestry of your angelic channeling, where the personal and the universal meet, merging into a single flow of love and service.

To understand this dynamic, it is important to know that there are two main types of angelic presences that can manifest throughout your channeling journey: personal angels and universal angels. Both are expressions of the same divine love, but present themselves in different ways and with different purposes.

Personal angels are those who walk with you from the beginning. They are presences that intertwine with your soul from before your first physical breath. They are with you in every incarnation, not as distant watchers, but as intimate companions, as silent witnesses of your evolution. They are not just guardians who prevent accidents or ward off dangers. They are part of your path, guardians of your deepest purpose. They know your fears, your weaknesses, your shadows—and yet, or for that very reason, they never turn away.

Your personal angel is not a neutral presence, bureaucratically designated at the moment of your conception. He chose to walk with you. And this choice arises from a vibrational affinity between your soul and his essence. There is something in you that resonates directly with this specific angel. He is not just your protector—he is your mirror in light. He reflects your potentialities, your forgotten virtues, and the spiritual talents that you brought with you to this life. Therefore, your personal angel is, at the same time, a guide and a mirror. He points the way, but, above all, reminds you of who you are.

Communication with the personal angel tends to be more intimate, more direct, because the connection between you is ancestral. This angel already knows your resistances, your recurring doubts, and your mechanisms of self-sabotage. He knows how to speak to you, adjusting the message so that it pierces your defenses with love and patience. Often, the presence of this angel is felt as something familiar, as if you were not meeting someone new, but rediscovering a forgotten part of yourself. And that is exactly it.

The personal angel does not change from one life to another, because he is not designated only to protect this specific existence. He protects your soul as a whole, accompanying it through the ups and downs of your complete evolutionary cycle. In different lives, you may perceive him in different ways—as a male figure, female, or as pure light. The form does not matter. The bond does.

Unlike the personal angel, universal angels do not belong to a particular soul. They are cosmic forces, divine intelligences that serve humanity as a whole. Each of them guards an essential quality of the Source—healing, protection, wisdom, love, courage, transmutation—and acts where that quality is needed, regardless of individual bonds. You can invoke Michael for protection even if you have never felt his presence before. Raphael can respond to a request for healing from someone who has never heard his name. Universal angels serve humanity without distinctions, without preferences.

These universal angels—or archangels, depending on tradition—have well-defined vibrational signatures. Each carries a specific color, frequency, and purpose. They are not "owners" of these qualities, but are perfect channels to express them. When you call on Chamuel, for example, you are not just asking for help from an external being, but tuning directly into the universal frequency of compassionate love. By invoking Uriel, you are adjusting your field to the golden flame of divine wisdom. These angels are living expressions of divine qualities, and their presence is felt in an expansive way, encompassing not only you, but the environment around you.

It is common, during the channeling process, to feel the presence of both types of angels. The personal angel is the one you feel almost as part of yourself—intimate, constant, familiar. He arrives in moments of internal crisis, in the silent dialogues between your heart and your soul. Universal angels arrive with a force that seems to come from outside, like a wave of light that spills over you and the environment. They arrive when your prayer surpasses the personal level and touches the collective—when your pain, your request, or your desire resonates with the pain and desire of many.

These universal angels can come and go, appear at specific moments and then move away, leaving only the trace of the divine quality they brought. They do not bind to your soul like the personal angel, but respond whenever your vibration tunes to theirs. It is an open connection, available to anyone with a sincere heart and clear intention.

With time and channeling practice, you will learn to differentiate these two types of presence. The personal angel is the golden thread that runs through your entire life, present even when you forget or doubt. Universal angels are like rays of sunlight that illuminate the way in critical moments, bringing specific qualities to fill your temporary gaps. Both are essential. One sustains, the other expands. One walks by your side, the other illuminates the horizon.

And, in the intertwining of these presences, your spiritual journey becomes a fluid dance between the intimate and the cosmic, between the personal and the universal. There are moments when the loving whisper of your personal angel is all you need—a gentle reminder that you have never been alone, even in the darkest nights of the soul. In others, it is the immense force of a universal angel that tears through the inner sky, bringing exactly the divine quality that was missing to sustain your next step. None of these presences replaces the other, because each fulfills an essential role within your expansion and your awakening.

Over time, you will realize that it is not the exact identification — the name, form, or hierarchy — that matters, but rather the delivery. The more you release the need to control with the mind, the deeper the connection becomes, and the clearer the purpose of each angelic visit. Your personal angel reminds you of your own brilliance, while the universal angels broaden your vision, showing you that your personal light is part of an infinite constellation of souls, all interconnected, all nourished by the same divine currents. This perception changes everything: you are not just protected or guided, you are a living link in the flow of creation itself.

And so, between intimate conversations with your guardian and sincere invocations to the universal angels, you learn to trust not only the messengers but also your own ability to listen. Because each angelic presence, whether personal or universal, does not arrive to take the place of your own light, but to remind you that this light already exists within you. And each time this reminder awakens, you gradually become a clearer, more rooted, and more conscious channel of the luminous vastness that always surrounds you — and that, deep down, is also what you are.

Chapter 14
The Golden Link

The connection between your soul and the angelic planes is a pulsating and continuous reality, a living current of energy that crosses the veil between worlds and intertwines with your deepest essence. It is not necessary to build this link from scratch or to conquer it through spiritual merits, as it is an intrinsic part of the structure of your being. From the instant your soul was conceived in the divine mind, this golden connection was woven, not as a privilege, but as a natural extension of your origin. Contact with angels, therefore, is not an extraordinary ability reserved for a chosen few; it is a vibrational memory that belongs to everyone, a dormant frequency that awaits only conscious recognition to awaken and blossom. Even when your mind is occupied with daily demands and allows itself to be swallowed by the pressures and noises of the physical world, this connection is never severed—it is merely covered by layers of forgetfulness, distraction, and forced self-sufficiency. Therefore, the first step to feeling this connection consciously is not to seek it outside, but to remember it within yourself.

This golden link is not a poetic metaphor; it is a real energetic structure, a vibrational bridge that starts from the center of your chest—or from even more subtle layers of your soul—and extends toward the higher spheres, where the angelic presence vibrates in its original purity. It is woven of intention, love, and recognition, and its strength does not depend on elaborate techniques or formal ceremonies, but on the quality of your inner presence. Every time you remember the existence of this bond, it shines a little brighter. Every time you turn to the angels, even amidst doubt or skepticism, the flow of this current intensifies. And, most importantly, every time you recognize that you are not separate from the light—that this connection is not something external, but an essential part of who you are—the link ceases to be a distant spiritual concept and becomes a tangible, almost physical, internal presence, sustaining your journey with a silent security.

Full awareness of this link is cultivated in the simplicity of daily encounters between you and the invisible. It is not necessary to wait for moments of deep meditation or solemn rituals to strengthen this connection. It is built in the instants when your heart spontaneously seeks comfort or guidance. When you close your eyes for a second, take a deep breath, and say, "I know you are here," something in that golden thread pulses more strongly. When you walk through nature and feel, effortlessly, a loving presence by your side, this link expands. When you write a sincere prayer or simply give thanks for something small, even without hearing a clear response, this current gains body and consistency. It is woven in subtle gestures, in silent words, and above all, in the loving repetition of the act of remembering. Remembering that you are accompanied. Remembering that separation is an illusion. Remembering that the light has never stopped flowing, only waited for your gaze to become visible.

With time and practice of this active remembrance, the golden link ceases to be an occasional connection and becomes a permanent foundation. It is no longer just a channel through which the angels reach you—it becomes the very backbone of your spiritual consciousness, an invisible axis that sustains your perception even in moments of doubt or disconnection. This link is your spiritual root, your channel of direct nourishment with the divine source and with the angelic presences that, more than messengers, are loving guardians of your original light. Creating this conscious connection is, ultimately, remembering that you have never been separated from what you seek. It is discovering that angels do not come from outside to illuminate your darkness—they emerge from within, as reflections of the light that has always existed in the core of your soul. And by recognizing this truth, the golden link is not only strengthened; it becomes part of your spiritual identity, a permanent bridge between your humanity and your divinity.

This golden link, as many channelers like to call it, is a living connection between you and the angelic plane. It is not a static line, but a constantly moving energy current, pulsing according to your emotions, your intentions, and your vibrational state. When you remember the presence of angels, this link shines more intensely. When you forget, it does not disappear, it merely retracts, waiting for your next conscious look. The link does not belong to the angels, nor does it belong to you. It is a third force, created by the sum of your intention and their loving presence. It is a soul bond, an energetic signature that unites your essence with theirs.

Creating this conscious connection is, therefore, much less a technical act and much more a state of being. It is not about performing rituals or uttering specific words, although these practices can help the mind focus. The true conscious connection is born when you choose, consistently, to live as someone who knows they are never alone. Each thought that recognizes the presence of angels, each prayer that is born spontaneously in your chest, each gesture of trust amidst fear, strengthens this link. It is built in the loving repetition of remembrance: they are here.

But how to transform this remembrance into something solid, tangible, that you can feel even on days when the fog of the world covers your perception? This is the heart of the conscious creation of the golden link. Angels do not demand your perfection, but your constancy. They do not need you to perceive them every day, but that you are willing, day after day, to open a sliver of consciousness through which they can enter. The golden link is not a chain forged in solemn rituals, but a subtle thread that strengthens in the sum of small daily encounters—the sigh of gratitude upon waking, the gesture of placing your hand on your chest before an important decision, the silent word of "help me" in the middle of a difficult conversation.

For this link to become conscious, it is essential that you personalize it. There is no universal formula, because each bond between soul and angel is unique. Perhaps for you this connection strengthens in moments of contemplative silence, looking at the sky or feeling the wind touch your skin. For another person, it may be in the act of lighting a candle or writing a letter of gratitude to the guardian angel. What matters is not the external form, but the internal coherence—the loving repetition of a gesture that, over time, becomes a permanent bridge between worlds.

Angels respond to your unique vibrational signature. Every time you call them, with your words, your tone of voice, your particular emotion, you adjust this golden link so that it resonates with who you are. It is not necessary to copy prayers from other people or try to imitate the way other channels connect. The link is yours. It carries your voice, your way of asking, your way of loving. And it is precisely this authenticity that makes it indestructible. A link built on external formulas is fragile, because it has no roots in who you really are. A link built on your truth, even if imperfect, is unbreakable.

Over time, this link becomes almost physical. You feel it as a constant presence, an invisible thread that starts from your chest or the top of your head and extends to something greater. In moments of calm, you perceive this thread as a slight pulsation, a warmth, or a subtle current passing through your body. In moments of crisis, it becomes a rescue cable, a golden bridge that holds you and pulls you back to the light. Creating a conscious connection with angels is not guaranteeing that you will never feel lost again. It is knowing, even in the midst of darkness, where to look.

This link is also a two-way street. It is not just you who connects to the angels—they also cross this bridge to reach you. Every time you open space to hear them, they adjust their frequency to become more perceptible to you. Not because they need to change—their light is constant—, but because they respect your rhythm. If you can only feel a slight warmth in your hands, they use that. If you better perceive external signs, they multiply them. They cross the golden link in the exact measure of your openness. And over time, this measure expands. Every small contact strengthens the next.

There is a moment, after many silent encounters, when the golden link ceases to be just a channeling tool and becomes a part of who you are. You no longer need to call them all the time because you know they are there. Not because you see or hear, but because the link is felt as an extension of your own being. This is the true purpose of the conscious connection: to dissolve the separation between you and them, until the angelic presence is no longer an external visit, but a constant reminder that the light has always dwelt within you.

This golden thread, woven between your soul and the angelic sphere, is not just a communication channel—it is a reflection of your own luminous essence. Every time you recognize your connection with the angels, you are also recognizing your innate connection with the Source, with the divine that pulsates in you and around you. The golden link is not something outside you, but an extension of your own spiritual heart. It is as if, by remembering the angels, you lit a spark that has always been within you, remembering that the divine has never been separate, only dormant beneath layers of forgetfulness.

Over time, this perception transforms the very way you walk through the world. The presence of angels, once felt in a real and intimate way, dissolves the fear of existential loneliness. You no longer seek desperate signs that something greater exists, because you begin to carry this certainty in your own body, as a vibration that is not lost even on the darkest days. The golden link becomes an invisible foundation, sustaining your choices, your words, your searches. Even when the senses fail or fatigue takes over, this silent current remains, pulsing in the background of every experience.

Over time, this perception transforms the very way you walk through the world. The presence of angels, once felt in a real and intimate way, dissolves the fear of existential loneliness. You no longer seek desperate signs that something greater exists, because you carry that certainty within your own body, like a vibration that doesn't fade even on the darkest days. The golden link becomes an invisible foundation, supporting your choices, your words, your searches. Even when your senses fail or weariness overcomes you, this silent current remains, pulsing in the depths of every experience.

And so, the journey of building this conscious link reveals itself, in fact, as the journey of returning to yourself. You discover that the angels were never distant, they were only waiting for the moment when you would be ready to see that they were always part of your own light. Not as something separate, but as a living reminder that, even amidst dense matter and the challenges of human existence, you never ceased to be a soul connected to the divine. The golden link, then, is not just a bridge to the angels—it is the golden reflection of what you have always been.

Chapter 15
Altered States and Subtle Trance

Angelic channeling unfolds from a delicate shift in the state of consciousness, where the habitual focus of the linear mind gives way to a broader, more refined, and receptive perception. This shift does not require the mind to shut down or the body to enter some kind of rigid immobility; on the contrary, it is a state of expanded presence in which you remain fully aware, but with a quality of attention that transcends ordinary logic. In this subtle state, your perception is not limited to physical senses or analytical thinking, but extends like vibrational antennas capable of picking up frequencies and impressions that exist beyond the visible. This border between wakefulness and the subtle is not something distant or mystical, but an accessible zone that your consciousness already knows and visits in spontaneous moments of introspection, creative daydreaming, or contemplative silence. The subtle trance is not an escape from reality, but an expansion of it — a widening of your field of perception, where angels can be felt, heard, and understood more clearly.

This altered state is, in essence, a subtle dance between relaxation and presence. The physical body, although relaxed, remains awake and available. The mind, although softened, stays alert enough to follow the flow of impressions that arise. It is as if you place yourself between worlds — without completely disconnecting from the material plane, but also without clinging exclusively to it. In this fluid boundary, your mental resistances dissolve and your natural perception of the subtle begins to reveal itself. The images, sensations, and words that emerge in this space are not artificial creations of the mind, but legitimate perceptions that your intuitive awareness captures as it attunes to the angelic frequency. The more you inhabit this space with naturalness and trust, the clearer and more fluid the messages become, because angels communicate through layers — images that carry emotions, emotions that convey words, words that awaken intuitions. Everything happens at the same time, in a web of meanings that can only be perceived when the logical mind becomes an observer rather than a controller.

Over time, the passage into this altered state becomes more organic, ceasing to be an isolated technique and integrating as a quality of presence that you carry into your daily life. You no longer need long preparations or formal rituals to open this door, because the constant practice itself dissolves the rigidity between the planes. The bridge between your ordinary mind and your expanded perception becomes so fluid that, in brief moments of silence or simple inner openness, the contact happens. This conscious permeability transforms channeling into something natural, accessible even in the pauses of everyday routine. You then realize that the true altered state is not an exotic condition reserved for special moments, but an extension of your own consciousness, an ever-present layer that only needs to be recognized to become available. And it is in this continuous state of openness and trust that the dialogue with the angels ceases to be a sporadic event and becomes an intimate, constant, subtle, and loving conversation — a natural flow between your heart and the luminous presence that has always been around you.

This altered state of consciousness is not an escape from reality. It is, in fact, an expansion of it. When you access this state, what happens is not the distancing of the rational mind, but the expansion of your focus. It is as if your field of perception widens, allowing you to perceive not only what is before your eyes but also what vibrates at the edges of the visible. The angels do not descend to you — it is you who gently rises to a meeting point between your world and theirs.

This altered state is natural. You have been in it many times without realizing it. Upon waking from a dream, in that instant when the mind has not yet fully taken control and you remember something but do not know if it is memory or vision. Or when you are deeply immersed in a creative activity, writing, painting, or dancing, and you lose track of time because something greater flows through you. These are moments of subtle trance, where your consciousness slips out of the ego's rigidity and becomes permeable to the subtle. Angelic channeling happens precisely in this space.

The challenge for many is to trust that these states are valid. Because we were taught to value the linear, logical, analytical mind. We were trained to distrust anything that cannot be weighed, measured, or proven. But angels do not live within these rules. They manifest in the space between thoughts, in the pause between inhalation and exhalation, at the border where mental control weakens and the heart takes command.

To consciously enter this altered state, the first step is to relax the body. The body is the first door. A tense, rigid, or overly tired body creates noise in the channel. It keeps you too anchored to the physical plane, like an anchor preventing flight. Relaxing the body opens space for subtle energy to flow. It does not need to be a deep relaxation, just a softening of habitual tension. The breath, slow and present, is your ally in this process.

After the body, the mind needs to be softened. It is not about forcing the mind to stop — this is a common mistake that only generates more resistance. The true altered state does not require absolute silence, but a shift of focus. Instead of trying to erase thoughts, you simply choose not to follow them. They pass, like clouds crossing the sky, but you do not need to grasp them. This softening of the mind is the second portal.

With the body and mind softened, the third portal opens: the opening to feeling. Here lies the real key to channeling. It is in this expanded state, where you are still aware but your perception has broadened, that angelic presence becomes perceptible. In the subtle trance, you do not lose control of yourself. You are not possessed by an external force. You remain present — but it is a different presence, broader, more receptive, as if every cell in you were listening.

Angels prefer this type of connection. They do not need you to shut down your consciousness to receive them. They prefer you to be present, whole, because true channeling is not just passive reception. It is a dialogue. You feel, perceive, respond. Even if there are no words, there is a vibrational dance between you and them. And this dance can only happen when you are awake enough to participate and relaxed enough to allow it.

This altered state, when practiced consistently, becomes more natural. In the beginning, you might need a small ritual to facilitate — lighting a candle, breathing deeply, listening to soft music. Over time, your body and mind learn the way. A single sigh, the closing of your eyes, and you already slip into that inner space where the subtle reveals itself. It is like opening a door you know well. Each time you pass through it, the crossing becomes easier.

Many people fear this altered state because they associate trance with something dangerous, a loss of control or an opening to unwanted energies. This is a remnant of cultural and religious fear. The subtle trance of angelic channeling is the opposite of that. It is a safe and loving expansion of your own consciousness, always within the limits you choose. Angels absolutely respect your free will. They do not invade, force, or take over. They only respond to your openness, as you offer it.

The more you trust this expanded state, the richer the communication becomes. Because angels speak in layers. The same message can come as a sensation in the body, an image in the mind, and an emotion in the heart, all at once. If you are present and receptive, you can capture these layers simultaneously. But if you are locked only in the logical mind, expecting clear and direct words, you miss much of what is being transmitted.

This altered state, therefore, is less a mystical trance and more a state of expanded presence. It is when you are neither completely in the physical plane nor completely out of it. You are between worlds, with one foot on each side, allowing the boundaries to dissolve. And when this expanded presence becomes your second nature, you realize that channeling angels is not a practice separate from your life. It is simply a different way of being present — more attentive, more open, more permeable to light.

Over time, the altered state dissolves into your life itself. You no longer need long preparations. You walk down the street and feel the presence. You are washing dishes and perceive a whisper. Because the subtle trance is not a distant place you need to reach. It is a quality of presence that seeps into the everyday, until your expanded perception becomes a natural part of who you are.

This walking between worlds, which at first may seem like a conscious effort, gradually reveals its true nature: a continuous flow between the visible and the invisible, between matter and the subtle. It is no longer an isolated practice confined to specific rituals, but a way of being in which each gesture and each silence carries the possibility of contact. This growing naturalness does not diminish the sacredness of the process — on the contrary, it expands the understanding that the sacred is not outside of ordinary life, but pulses in every moment lived with openness and surrender.

With this increasing familiarity, you learn to recognize the subtlest signs of presence — those slight changes in the air, the rhythm of your breath, or the inner texture of silence. The line between the altered state and everyday life becomes thin, almost nonexistent, until you realize that the true channel is not a moment or a method, but your very being — permeable and receptive.

The dialogue with the angels ceases to be an event marked by a beginning and an end, and becomes an ongoing conversation, interrupted only by the inevitable distractions of the human mind.

And so, in this weaving of worlds, angelic channeling transforms into a companion presence — gentle, constant, and loving. Not as a separate voice echoing from afar, but as an internal vibration that accompanies your steps and your pauses.

Channeling angels is no longer something you do — it becomes something you are: a living bridge where the divine and the human touch, where your consciousness expands, and your soul learns to listen.

Chapter 16
Recording Contacts

The relationship established between you and the angels manifests as a subtle field of communication that transcends the ordinary and is rooted in the daily practice of attention, presence, and surrender. Each contact, however brief or ethereal it may seem, constitutes a fundamental piece in the mosaic of this developing connection. It is in this intertwining of sensory perceptions, delicate intuitions, and glimpses of the invisible that the practice of recording assumes a much greater role than the simple annotation of occurrences: it becomes the concrete support of a bridge between worlds. Recording each sensation, each internal word, each fragment of image or energy that comes to you is the act of giving density to what, otherwise, would dissipate like a breeze. This conscious choice to document is the first demonstration of commitment to the developing bond. By putting on paper or recordings what emerges during channelings, you communicate to the universe and yourself that this communication is valid, that it has value and deserves to be preserved establishes a symbolic and energetic foundation for this exchange to deepen over time.

The moment you are willing to record your interactions with the angels, a silent process of maturing your inner listening begins. Each word written or recorded ceases to be just an echo of the moment lived and begins to act as a vibrational anchor, fixing in the material plane an experience that originally manifested in subtle layers of consciousness. This record becomes a testimony to your openness, your willingness to welcome what comes from spiritual dimensions, even when the linear mind hesitates to give credence to what cannot be immediately proven. By writing, you not only remember, but reinforce the very reality of the experience. And this reality, sustained by the act of recording, gains solidity and continuity. With each annotation, you reaffirm to yourself that these presences are real, that dialogue is possible and that the construction of this relationship occurs in the field of constancy — where each small documented detail is a seed, which may or may not reveal its importance in the future, but which, even so, already fulfills the function of nourishing the soil of your spiritual path.

As the channeling diary grows in pages and records, it begins to reflect not only what was received, but the very journey of transformation of the one who writes. Each recorded contact carries within it not only the message of the angels, but the response of the channel — the doubts, the initial perceptions, the resistances that arose and, over time, were softened or understood. This diary, then, is not just a space of spiritual memory; it becomes a mirror where you, by rereading your own words, find not only the angels, but the version of yourself who dared to listen to the invisible. It is, at the same time, testimony and tool of self-knowledge, as it highlights the unique rhythm with which your sensitivity unfolds, with which your certainties are rebuilt, and with which your confidence matures. In the rhythm between receiving and recording, a silent pact arises between you and the sacred: a commitment to listen more finely, to honor each sign and to give body to what, without this record, could be forgotten or minimized. The diary, therefore, becomes not only the record of spiritual contacts, but the very map of the construction of a bond, where the visible and the invisible meet, and where your soul learns to recognize, honor, and keep each whisper as an essential part of your own history.

Recording your perceptions, even those that seem insignificant, is a way to give body to the invisible. The moment you write or record your experiences, you anchor the light you received in the material plane. You transform subtle impressions into concrete words, and this process, by itself, deepens the connection. Writing is a bridge between the inner and outer worlds, and the act of recording your contacts with the angels is a symbolic gesture that you value this bond. It is like saying to them: "I am listening. I am paying attention. I want to remember."

In the first contacts, the mind may try to minimize or question what was felt. Without the record, these experiences often get lost in the whirlwind of days. That soft image that arose during meditation, that warm feeling in the hands, that sweet whisper that almost went unnoticed — all this is easily swept away by routine if it is not anchored. The diary is your fertile ground, where each of these seeds of light can be planted, nurtured and, over time, understood in depth.

More than a record book, the channel's diary is a mirror. When you go back and reread your notes weeks or months later, you will notice something curious: the angels build long dialogues, which do not always fit in a single session or contact. An image received in January can connect with a phrase whispered in April, which in turn resonates with a childhood dream that you wrote down without giving importance. Angels have infinite patience to tell a story, and that story is yours. But only those who record are able to perceive the golden thread that connects each chapter of this narrative.

There is no single or right way to record. Some people feel comfortable writing long reports, detailing every nuance of the experience. Others prefer to write down loose words, brief sensations, symbols that arose without explanation. There are those who prefer to draw — sketching the images they saw internally — and there are those who record their voice, narrating what they felt soon after contact. The format is personal. What matters is creating the habit of giving form to the experience, of not letting the subtle get lost in oblivion.

Over time, the diary becomes a map. It reveals patterns, cycles, recurring messages. You begin to notice that certain themes come back repeatedly — healing fear, strengthening confidence, rescuing your essential truth. Angels are masters at repeating what your soul needs to hear, until you not only understand with the mind, but feel with your whole being. Without a record, these repetitions can seem like isolated coincidences. With the diary, they become a living tapestry, a confirmation that you are being guided with love and patience.

Recording is also an antidote against doubt. On days when the connection seems distant, when the mind questions whether everything was just imagination or desire, rereading your own words is a powerful reminder. It is proof that there was contact, that something greater crossed the veil and touched your consciousness. It is a testimony that you leave for yourself, like a letter written by a more open and confident version of who you are, to be read on days when that confidence wavers.

The angels, when they perceive your effort to record, also adjust their communication. They know you are paying attention, and begin to transmit their messages with more clarity and continuity. Not because they need to be formalized in a diary, but because they understand that you are building a real bridge, which does not depend only on fleeting memory, but on a firm commitment to honor each contact. Recording is honoring. It is saying: "This presence is important to me. This dialogue deserves to be preserved."

Another powerful aspect of the channeling diary is that it not only serves to record the messages received, but also to document your own internal process. Each emotion that arises during channeling, each doubt, each resistance or fear is part of building that bond. Angels do not just want you to listen — they want you to know yourself through what you hear. By recording not only what came from them, but also what came from you, your diary becomes a mirror of your own journey of spiritual openness and maturity.

Over time, this record becomes sacred. It is not just a notebook or digital file. It is an altar of words, where each phrase keeps a little of the presence you felt. And when you reread your own notes, you not only remember the message — you relive the vibration of the moment. Words, when written with presence and truth, keep within them the frequency of that instant. By reading, you not only understand. You feel again.

Some worry about recording everything perfectly, with carefully chosen words. But angels do not expect literature from you. They expect truth. If the only word you can write after contact is "peace," that is enough. Because that word, written in the heat of the experience, carries the vibration of that peace. The diary is not about producing a book of spirituality. It is about creating a vibrational timeline, a golden thread where each small contact is recorded as a pearl.

Over the years, the channel diary becomes something precious. It tells the story of your relationship with the invisible. It reveals how your perception was refined, how your doubts turned into confidence, how the presence of angels gradually ceased to be an extraordinary event to become a natural part of your life. It is the record of a love story — between you and the divine, between your soul and those who came to remind you of who you are.

And it is precisely in this intertwining of words and presences that the diary ceases to be just a record to become a space of revelation. As the days pass and the pages accumulate, you will realize that you are not just writing about the angels — you are writing about who you become when you allow them to walk by your side. Each annotation is a mark of this subtle meeting between worlds, a delicate seam between the visible and the invisible, between your voice and the light breath that blows through you.

Over time, the very act of recording becomes a spiritual practice. It's no longer about keeping memories, but about anchoring presences. By writing, you reaffirm your place in this continuous dialogue, acknowledging your ability to listen and be heard. The journal, then, is both a reflection of what came from outside and proof that within you there is fertile space, ready to welcome each new message. It registers not only contacts, but the construction of a trust that, like every true relationship, matures in invisible layers.

And when, at some point, you reread your own words with the eyes of someone who has traveled a long road, you will recognize there more than records of spiritual encounters. You will see the portrait of your own growth, of your listening becoming finer, of your soul learning to decipher whispers. Each line will hold not only memories, but presences. And so, between pages and silences, your journal will become silent proof that the divine was never distant — it was just waiting for a safe space to reveal itself.

Chapter 17
Angelic Symbols and Signatures

Delving deeper into the connection with angels reveals a dimension where conventional language gives way to more subtle and direct forms of communication, shaped by symbols and energetic signatures that transcend linear logic. These symbols, far from being mere visual adornments, manifest as vibrational condensations, where each line, each color, and each form carries a specific frequency. Angelic presence, as it approaches, is not only revealed by whispered words or faint sensations, but also by images that are etched into the inner mind, visual echoes of an ancestral communication that predates written and spoken language. These symbols are not chosen at random; they emerge as reflections of the unique essence of each angel, energetic impressions that translate their spiritual signature and their specific purpose within the established bond. By recognizing and welcoming these symbols, the channel not only receives messages, but establishes a direct vibrational dialogue, where the soul responds even before the mind seeks comprehension.

This symbolic language acts as a living bridge between worlds, connecting the subtle and invisible plane to the concrete space of conscious perception.

Each light-filled symbol is a gateway, a vibrational key that opens not only the connection with the emitting angel, but also with deep layers of the channel's own spiritual consciousness. When receiving a symbol during a channeling session, the mind may hesitate, seeking known meanings or logical associations, but true understanding occurs at a deeper level, where the soul immediately recognizes the frequency embedded in the received form. Each curve and each sparkle act as memory codes, awakening dormant memories and activating parts of the being that often remain unexplored in the common routine. The symbol ceases to be just a visual record and begins to act as a vibrational mirror, reflecting not only the angelic presence, but also the internal state of the receiver, creating a resonance dance between emitter and receiver.

With time and consistent practice, these symbols become more than fleeting records of spiritual contacts; they begin to form a true language of their own between channel and angel. Each symbol carries within it a vibrational memory, and each time the gaze rests upon it, the original connection is reactivated. Storing, drawing, and revisiting these symbols therefore becomes a practice of conscious reconnection, an exercise in anchoring the subtle presence in everyday material life. The symbol notebook, filled with strokes, shapes, and colors, transforms into a unique spiritual map, where each page holds not only records of contacts, but also testimonies of the maturation of the channel's own sensitivity. Each symbol, filled with intention and reverence, acts as an active portal, reminding the channel that communication with the sacred is continuous and fluid, even when the rational mind forgets. This visual, living, and pulsating language transforms into an intimate vocabulary between the visible and the invisible, where each form is a call and each presence is a confirmation that the spiritual journey is accompanied and sustained at every step.

Angels love to work with symbols because they bypass the filters of the rational mind. Unlike words, which can be questioned, doubted, and reinterpreted according to beliefs and fears, symbols enter directly into the subtle field. They activate ancient memories, touch places of consciousness that are not always accessible to linear thinking. A symbol received in a channeling session is not just a pretty image — it is a vibrational key. It holds within itself a unique energetic signature, which connects you to the angel or to the specific frequency it carries.

Each angel has its own vibrational signature. This signature can manifest as a predominant color, a specific geometric shape, or even as a luminous pattern that arises spontaneously during contact. Some channels see golden spirals, others perceive light flowers or shimmering constellations that appear in the internal space of the mind. The exact form does not matter — what matters is that each symbol is a mark of presence. It is as if each angel leaves their "energetic calling card," a subtle impression that you can access whenever you want to reconnect with that specific presence.

These symbolic signatures are not just artistic forms. They are vibrational portals. When you draw or visualize a received symbol, you are recreating the vibrational field of that angel. The symbol is an anchor. It calls back the presence, because it carries within itself the essence of the original connection. Therefore, keeping these symbols, drawing them in your diary or altar, or even carrying them with you in the form of an amulet or jewel, is a powerful way to keep the connection open. The symbol is a physical reminder of an invisible presence, and each time your eyes land on it, the bond is reinforced.

Angels can offer symbols in different ways. Some arise spontaneously during channeling sessions — you close your eyes and a specific form draws itself on the mind's screen. Others can come through dreams, imprinted in light over dreamlike scenarios. There are cases where the symbol is revealed through synchronicities — you think of your angel and, hours later, you find the same symbol in a book, on a sign, or in the pattern of a cloud. Angels use symbolic language to reaffirm their constant presence, even when you are not in a state of formal channeling.

These symbols can also function as seals of protection. When you draw or visualize a channeled symbol, you are not only invoking the angel's presence — you are surrounding your field with their vibration. Each stroke, each curve, or angle carries a specific coding. Even if you do not intellectually understand the exact meaning, your soul knows. Your energy responds. Because these symbols are not just spiritual decorations.

They are instruments of vibrational harmonization, as effective as a prayer or a direct invocation.

Over time, you will notice that symbols do not just arrive to identify angels. They are also condensed messages. A received symbol can contain an entire answer, a complete teaching, a specific reminder that your soul needs at that moment. Sometimes, angels prefer to send symbols instead of words because they know that, through the mind, the message could be distorted. The symbol is pure — it arrives without interference, straight to the heart.

The process of learning to decode these symbols is part of the channel's maturity. In the beginning, there may be anxiety to immediately understand what each form means. The mind wants to translate, to fit into known meanings. But true symbolic understanding is experiential. You do not understand the symbol only with the mind — you feel, perceive, and allow it to reveal its meaning little by little, in layers. Each time you look at a channeled symbol, something new can be revealed. Because angelic symbols are alive. They are not static — they are dynamic portals that respond to your own expansion of consciousness.

Some channels receive personal symbols, exclusive to their journey. These are unique signatures, created between you and your personal angel, which function as master keys to access deeper levels of connection. Other times, the symbols are universal, belonging to the spiritual tradition of humanity. The six-pointed star, the golden spiral, the flower of life — all these are symbols that carry collective layers of wisdom, accessible to any channel attuned with light.

The most important thing when receiving a symbol is to trust what came. Even if it seems too simple or without immediate meaning, it carries a hidden meaning that will be revealed at the right time. Often, channeled symbols anticipate information that your mind is not yet ready to understand. They are seeds planted in your field, and each practice, each prayer, each moment of openness waters that seed until it blooms into spontaneous understanding.

Keeping these symbols is keeping maps of your own journey. Each one is a footprint of your angel on your path, a reminder that each step is accompanied. Creating a specific notebook just for these symbols can be a powerful practice. Drawing, painting, embroidering, or sculpting these forms is a way to anchor their energy in the physical plane. It is not just art — it is light magic. By giving body to an angelic symbol, you not only reinforce the bond with your angel, but anchor in your physical space a frequency that acts even when you are not looking.

Over time, you will be able to recognize which angel is approaching just by the shape or color that arises even before any word. This symbolic language will become part of your expanded sensitivity. And just as we learn to speak a new language by hearing it and practicing it, you will learn to "speak" the angelic symbolic language by living with it, drawing it, dreaming with it, allowing each symbol to reveal its secret at the right time.

Over time, this coexistence with symbols becomes almost a silent dance between you and the subtle world. Without needing to force or seek, they begin to arise at the most unexpected moments, like discreet nods from the angels reminding you that communication remains alive, even on ordinary days. The screen of the mind becomes receptive to these appearances, and you begin to recognize not only the strokes and shapes, but the exact vibration of each presence that announces itself even before any word is spoken.

And it is precisely in this naturalness that symbols reveal their greatest strength. They cease to be just received images to become part of your intimate spiritual vocabulary — a silent language that asks for no explanations, only space to be felt. Each curve or sparkle imprinted on the mind is a kind of call, an invitation to step out of linear thinking and into direct perception, where the soul understands what the mind cannot yet name.

The symbolic universe becomes a living bridge between worlds, a luminous calligraphy written on the fabric of the invisible. Each symbol kept, drawn, or simply remembered is an open door, a frequency anchored in your personal field. And it is in this constant encounter between the visible and the invisible that the channel strengthens, learning that each form is a presence, and each presence is a promise that you never walk alone.

Chapter 18
Personal Angelic Name

The personal angelic name emerges as an ancestral whisper, echoing through the layers of time and existences, traversing veils of forgetfulness until it gently lands in the consciousness of the one who is ready to hear it. More than a designation or a spiritual title, this name reveals itself as a vibrational key that translates the unique essence of the connection between the human soul and the angelic presence that accompanies it from the first breaths of its spiritual journey. This name is not something external that is discovered by chance or chosen by affinity; it is a memory dormant within one's own being, a singular note of the invisible symphony that connects each soul to its primordial guardian. It is the sonorous reflection of a bond that precedes this existence and extends beyond it, involving soul and angel in a continuous dance of recognition and protection.

Each angel bearing a personal name is not just an external presence that approaches or departs according to human will. It is a living extension of the divine consciousness that chose, from the beginning, to accompany and illuminate the specific path of a particular soul. This angelic name, therefore, is not just a word or an arbitrary sound sequence. It is a coded frequency that resonates simultaneously with the essence of the angel and with the unique spiritual signature of that soul whom it assists. It is as if each soul and its angel shared a specific tone within the vast cosmic melody, a tone that, when pronounced or felt internally, instantly triggers the memory of the original unity between them. When the name arises, whether in a dream, in a meditative whisper, or as a lightning intuition, it does not come as a novelty, but as a memory that awakens something that has always been present—a loving echo of the spiritual home shared between angel and soul.

Recognizing the name of your personal angel is not a mere exercise of identification or mystical curiosity; it is a milestone of maturation of inner listening and readiness for direct dialogue between the visible and the invisible. This name, once revealed, does not act as a magic formula or a command word. It is, first and foremost, a vibrational bridge that strengthens trust and dissolves the illusory separation between the seeker and the one who has always been present. Pronouncing this name, silently or aloud, is like aligning oneself to a specific subtle frequency, allowing the angelic presence to become more tangible, not because it approached, but because the channel opened. This name, therefore, is not an external element to be conquered, but an internal memory to be unveiled, a key that has always been in the hands of the soul, awaiting only the moment when it was mature enough to recognize the golden glow emanating from its own interior.

Angels do not have names like humans. They do not need words to identify each other. In the plane they inhabit, each angel is known by its vibration—a unique set of light, sound, and purpose. For them, their names are like songs. They are not fixed words, but living melodies, which change slightly as they serve and evolve. However, when they approach the human plane, when they wish to create a more direct and intimate bond with someone, they translate this essential melody into something our mind can understand: a name.

This name is not given at random. It is carefully adjusted to your personal vibration. It is as if the angel immersed itself in the light of your soul and chose, within its own essence, a frequency that echoes with yours. Therefore, the personal angelic name is both a key and a mirror. It is a bridge between you and this being of light, but it is also a revelation of a forgotten part of yourself. Knowing your angel's name is, in a way, remembering your own spiritual name—the one that existed before any earthly identity.

The personal angelic name does not need to be received immediately. In fact, angels often wait for the right moment to reveal their names. They know that if the name comes before the connection is mature, the human mind can transform this revelation into a fetish or an anxious search for evidence and validations. The name only reveals itself when you are ready to receive it with your heart, and not just with the curiosity of the mind. This moment is subtle, and often happens when you least expect it—during meditation, in a dream, or even in the middle of a common activity, when the mind is relaxed and open.

Many people wonder how to know if the name received is real or if it was fabricated by their own mind. This doubt is understandable, but angels have a loving way of responding. When the name is legitimate, it resonates. It lands within you as something that already existed and was suddenly remembered. There is a deep, almost physical recognition. The heart responds. It is as if a forgotten note of an old song was played, and you, even without remembering the entire song, know that that note belongs to you.

The personal angelic name, once received, becomes a vibrational key. Pronouncing it aloud is a way to activate this connection, as if each time you said the name, the bridge between your world and theirs became firmer. But it is important to remember: the name is not a magic word, not a control formula. It is not the name that commands the angel—it is the love and attunement that you build with it. The name is a door, but it is your heart that opens or closes that door.

There are also cases where the name arrives fragmented, like an incomplete sound or a loose syllable. This does not mean an error. It means that the channel is adjusting to capture the complete signature. And, in some cases, the full name may be revealed over years, as the relationship between you and the angel matures. Angels are in no hurry. They know that true connection does not rush—it blooms at the right time, like a flower that blossoms under the right light.

Another common doubt is whether the name needs to be in a sacred or ancient language. The answer is no. The personal angelic name can come in any language, or in no known language. It can be a combination of sounds that makes no logical sense, but that carries a vibration that your soul recognizes. Angels are not tied to human languages. They translate their signatures into sounds that your mind is capable of processing—and this can vary according to your culture, your sensitivity, and your own spiritual history.

Receiving your angel's name is not a privilege reserved for a few. Anyone who cultivates openness and a sincere desire to build this relationship can receive this gift. But it is essential to remember: the name is a gift, not a goal. It does not define your ability to channel, nor does it determine the depth of the connection. There are people who channel their angels throughout their lives without ever knowing their names, and this does not make the relationship less true or less sacred. The name is a loving detail, but the true bond is silent, made of presence, trust, and surrender.

After the name is received, you can use it in your prayers, meditations, and even in internal dialogues. Calling them by name is a way of recognizing the individuality of this presence that walks with you. But angels do not need to be named to respond. Even without a name, they hear every prayer, feel every emotion, and respond to every sincere sigh. The name is a gift to you, not to them. It is an anchor for your mind, a way to make tangible a presence that, by nature, is infinite.

As the relationship deepens, the personal angelic name can evolve. Some channels receive new variations, new sounds, or complementary titles as their own vibration expands. This does not mean that the angel has changed, but that the relationship between you has gained new layers, and the name accompanies this expansion. It is a living dance between soul and light, between human and divine.

Understanding the personal angelic name as a living part of this dance is to free yourself from the need to control it or decipher it completely. The name is not a key that opens all doors at once, but a melody that is played in fragments, as you walk with your angel through the subtle territories of the soul. It pulsates like an ancestral echo, reminding that each sound is only the visible tip of a much larger frequency—a frequency that resonates not only with your angel, but with what is most essential in you.

And it is in this space of silent recognition, where the mind gives way to presence, that the name ceases to be just information and becomes a kind of natural prayer. Calling it is not just invoking an external presence, but remembering a forgotten part of yourself, a luminous identity that pulsates along with your soul from the beginning. Every time you pronounce this name aloud or just feel it vibrate within your chest, you reinforce the golden thread that connects you—a thread that crosses time, forms, and the veils between worlds.

In the end, the name is less a possession and more an encounter. It is a bridge that you cross as many times as necessary, until, one day, you realize that it is no longer necessary to call. The presence already lives in you, without distance or formality. The name, then, dissolves into the relationship itself, and what remains is pure recognition: the angel and you have always been parts of the same song. You were just waiting for the right moment to be heard together.

Chapter 19
Channeled Writing

Channeled writing presents itself as a sacred practice where the barrier between worlds dissolves, and the conscious mind becomes a silent receptacle for the direct transmission of angelic consciousness. More than a creative exercise or a search for inspiration, it represents an act of profound surrender, where the ego gives way to the subtle presence, allowing communication to flow without filters, without judgments, and without the need to understand or control what arrives. Each word recorded in this state carries a specific vibration, an energetic signature that transcends the immediate meaning of the phrases and reaches directly the subtlest layers of the soul. It is not just about recording spiritual messages, but about opening a resonance field where light condenses into words and angelic presence finds a dwelling in the materiality of writing. By allowing this current of consciousness to express itself freely, the channeler discovers that the very act of writing becomes a ritual of alliance and trust, where each written word is a gesture of welcome and each filled page is a living bridge between dimensions.

This flow of communication, when free of mental interference, manifests naturally, fluidly, and often surprisingly. The channeler does not "think" what they write, nor plan or previously structure the content. The words arrive like an invisible current, already formed, just waiting to be anchored on paper or screen. Each term carries vibrational precision, even when the immediate meaning is not fully understood. The conscious mind is invited to occupy a secondary role, becoming a kind of silent observer who merely witnesses the emergence of something greater, without trying to interpret or shape the message according to their own beliefs or expectations. It is in this space of non-control, where linear thinking withdraws and the heart takes over the listening, that channeled writing reveals its true nature: a direct dialogue between angelic intelligence and the divine essence that inhabits every human being.

With constant practice, the channeler learns to recognize the unique texture of these transmissions. Unlike common or even inspired writing, channeled writing has its own cadence, a fluidity that is independent of the emotional or intellectual state of the moment. Even when the mind doubts or questions the authenticity of what is being recorded, the vibration imprinted in the text carries a kind of energetic signature that, when reread later, resonates as a silent reminder that that communication came from a space beyond the common mind. This vibration can be felt in the lightness of the words, in the unexpected clarity of the answers, and, especially, in the effect that the message has on the channeler themselves. More than providing information or practical advice, channeled writing acts as an instrument of inner realignment, where the energy of angelic presence is incorporated directly through the words. Each record becomes not only a message to be understood, but a vibrational anchor that sustains and expands the field of connection between the channeler and their spiritual guides.

Inspired writing and channeled writing are sibling processes, but not identical. Both are born from an inner space of openness, receptive silence, and sensitive listening. But they follow different paths within the writer. Inspired writing is like a light breeze that crosses the mind and heart, awakening ideas, phrases, and reflections that flow naturally, as if they were already ready and only needed to find the surface of the paper. It is born from the soul and the subtle contact with its own internal wisdom, often amplified by the presence of angels, but without this presence manifesting clearly or directly. Inspired writing is like listening to a distant music, whose notes awaken memories and truths stored within you.

Channeled writing, however, is different. In it, the channeler is not just inspired—they become a direct means of transmission. The angelic presence not only whispers or inspires, but dictates, guides, and conducts. The channeler remains conscious, but clearly feels that the words that flow do not originate from the common mind, nor from personal reflection. They arrive as a continuous current, coming from a space that the channeler recognizes as external and at the same time deeply intimate. The sensation is of opening space within oneself for a loving, wise, and familiar voice to take the lead and guide the hand, the words, and even the rhythm of breathing.

In inspired writing, you feel that you are writing, only in a more fluid and creative state. In channeled writing, you feel that something greater is writing through you. Your role is only to allow. Not to interpret, not to correct, not to edit—just to let the current flow. In the beginning, this may seem strange, even uncomfortable for the mind accustomed to controlling the creative process. But, over time, you learn to recognize the vibrational signature of angelic presence and to trust that, even without understanding every word at the moment it arises, there is a greater wisdom guiding the flow.

Angels like to use channeled writing because it is a safe form of communication. Unlike clairaudience, which can be easily confused with one's own thoughts, writing leaves a clear record. Even if you doubt what you received at the moment, you can come back later, reread, and perceive layers of meaning that were invisible at the time of reception. Channeled writing is like an echo of invisible dialogue, preserved in time and available to be revisited whenever necessary.

This process does not require special talent. Anyone who has a sincere desire to connect and the willingness to empty themselves to serve as a channel can experience channeled writing. It is not necessary to have perfect handwriting or to be a writer by vocation. The value of the message is not in the aesthetics of the text, but in the purity of the transmission. Some messages arrive fragmented, others flow like continuous rivers of words. Some are simple and direct, others are poetic and full of symbolic images. Everything depends on the frequency of the communicating angel, the channeler's state, and the nature of the message that needs to be delivered.

The mind, especially in the first contacts, tends to interfere. It questions: "Am I making this up? Am I just writing what I want to hear?" This doubt is part of the process. Angels are not offended by it. They know that trust is built in practice, in the loving repetition of opening space and allowing something greater to manifest. The most reliable test of the authenticity of channeled writing is the vibration it leaves. If, when rereading, you feel peace, clarity, tenderness, or a greater truth than you would be able to write on your own, then there is angelic presence there.

Another way to distinguish channeled writing is to observe how it flows. Common writing requires effort, searching for words, constant revisions. Channeled writing has its own rhythm, almost automatic. The words arrive even before they are thought of, as if they were already in the air, just waiting for someone to capture them. The channeler is often surprised by what they wrote, as if the words had passed through their hands without asking permission. This fluidity is one of the hallmarks of angelic presence.

Angels also use channeled writing as a tool for healing. Often, they guide the channeler to write to themselves, messages of encouragement, forgiveness, or guidance. These messages are like love letters from your divine essence to your human part. They touch wounds that the mind cannot reach, dissolve old fears, and recall forgotten truths. It is not uncommon for the channeler to cry while writing, because the very vibration of the channeled words is therapeutic. Each phrase carries a healing frequency, as if the angel's light were imprinted in each letter.

Over time, the channeler learns to flow between inspired and channeled writing naturally. At times, the writing is born from the soul, echoing the inner wisdom awakened by angelic contact. At others, it comes directly from the angel, as a pure transmission. There is no rigid boundary between one and the other. Both are expressions of the same subtle dance between your consciousness and the presence of angels. The difference is only the degree of mind interference. In inspired writing, the mind still participates. In channeled, it observes from afar, while the heart takes command.

Creating an exclusive notebook for your inspired and channeled writings is a powerful way to honor this bond. Each page is an altar where the sacred manifests in the form of a word. When rereading these messages, you will realize that many of them are not just answers to specific questions—they are eternal reminders. They are fragments of wisdom that, even after years, remain alive, vibrating on paper as if they had been written yesterday. Because the channeled word is like that: timeless. It transcends time, carrying with it the presence of the one who breathed it.

Over time, the act of channeling writing becomes more than a spiritual practice—it reveals itself as a continuous dialogue between the soul and the divine, a safe space where intimate questions find answers that often arrive before they are formulated. Each new contact through words deepens not only the trust in the bond with the angels, but also the recognition that this communication is, in essence, a reminder of something ancestral: the natural ability of the human soul to talk with the light.

And it is in this space of silent surrender that channeled writing gradually dissolves the boundary between who asks and who answers. The messages that arrive are no longer just external advice or guidance, but echoes of one's own inner wisdom, awakened and brought to the surface by the loving presence of angels. Each written page becomes not only a record of communication between worlds, but also a living testimony of how human consciousness expands when it trusts, listens, and allows itself to be an instrument of the subtle.

When rereading these words years later, you will realize that they hold hidden layers—messages that were not visible at the time of writing, but that now shine clearly. This is the true legacy of channeled writing: more than answers, it offers doors. Doors to new understandings, to reunions with forgotten parts of oneself, and to the permanent memory that, in every word breathed from the invisible, the sacred has always found a way to say: "I am here."

Chapter 20
Inner Voice and Angelic Voice

Listening to the angelic voice stems from the gradual construction of an inner space where the mind yields to subtle perception and where the soul becomes receptive to the vibration that crosses the veils between dimensions. Differentiating the voice of one's own mind from the voice of an angel is not a technical or linear process, but a journey of inner attunement, where each layer of consciousness is invited to recognize patterns, textures, and frequencies that do not belong to the common flow of daily thoughts. The human mind, with its constant analytical activity and incessant narratives, is accustomed to occupying the entire field of perception. Its inner voices reflect accumulated experiences, learned beliefs, and defense mechanisms shaped throughout life. These voices echo concerns, desires, fears, and personal stories, composing the tangle of mental sounds that fill most of the day. The angelic voice, however, slips between these noises without competing for space, manifesting as a subtle thread, an almost imperceptible breath that stands out precisely for its absence of tension, urgency, or repetition. It does not struggle to be heard; it simply is—available, present, and vibrating at a frequency of love and clarity that is revealed to the attentive heart.

The tone of the angelic voice is marked by a firm softness, a serenity that does not depend on logical explanations to be recognized as true. Even when it conveys challenging messages or guides the channel to face their own shadows, it does so without carrying any judgment or reactive emotional charge. While the voice of the mind often reflects insecurities, conditioned opinions, and impulses of self-protection, the angelic voice is pure presence, free of emotional contamination and hidden agendas. Its sole intention is to guide, illuminate, and remind the divine essence of the one who listens. This absence of pressure or expectation, this loving invitation that does not require an immediate response, is one of the clearest marks of angelic presence. Even when the mind tries to interfere, question, or seek proof, the vibration of this voice remains intact—undisturbed as a silent lake that only reflects, without retaining or distorting the light that touches it.

True discernment between the inner voice and the angelic voice matures as the channel develops trust in their own ability to listen beyond thoughts. This requires practice, silence, and a sincere willingness to recognize when the mind is trying to take command. In the beginning, it is common for angelic messages to arrive mixed with personal impressions, reflections of expectations, and unconscious projections. But, over time, the vibrational signature of each angel begins to become as familiar as the voice of an intimate friend.

Each angel possesses a unique timbre, a unique way of manifesting—whether through words, images, sensations, or even a simple wave of peace that fills the environment. The more constant the contact, the clearer this signature becomes, and the easier it becomes to distinguish the subtle vibrational perfume of an angelic presence amidst the turmoil of the mind. This recognition does not come from mental effort, but from spiritual intimacy—from the daily construction of a relationship where the soul, the mind, and the angels learn to share the same inner space, in harmony and trust.

The human mind is a constant whirlwind of thoughts, inner dialogues, memories, and projections. It is a powerful tool, capable of creating, analyzing, and solving complex problems. But, at the same time, it is also an inexhaustible source of noise, which often hinders the clarity of connection with the angelic plane. The mind, by its nature, questions, doubts, and seeks to fit everything into logical and known patterns. And the angels, in turn, inhabit a space that transcends linear logic. They speak in intuitions, in sensations, in impulses that do not always make immediate sense to the rational mind.

When you open yourself to channeling, it is natural for the mind to try to actively participate in the process. It wants to interpret, translate, compare with its expectations and beliefs. And it is exactly at this point that confusion can arise. If you are not attentive, you may end up confusing your own thoughts and desires with the angelic message. You may end up interpreting your own anxieties as divine signs, or, conversely, discarding genuine intuitions as "just something in your head."

The first key to discerning between the inner voice and the angelic voice is to recognize the difference in texture between them. The voice of the mind is familiar. It is made up of your usual inner dialogues, the tone of voice you use to speak to yourself, the words and expressions that are part of your mental vocabulary. It is linear, sequential, and often accompanied by images and emotions that you recognize as your own. The angelic voice, on the other hand, has a different texture. It is softer, more subtle, like a thread of silk that crosses the rough fabric of your thoughts. It does not shout, does not impose itself, does not demand attention. It simply presents itself, like a melody that you recognize, but do not know where it came from.

This angelic voice can arrive in different ways. For some, it manifests as a sudden intuition, a clarity that springs from nowhere, without logical reasoning. For others, it arises as an inner voice, but with a different tone from yours—sweeter, firmer, or with a quality that you cannot define, but recognize as different from your own. There are those who perceive it as a symbolic image, which carries a complete message, or as a pure emotion—love, peace, compassion—that fills the inner space without a defined origin.

The second key to discerning is to observe the frequency of the message. The mind, however positive it tries to be, often carries a hint of anxiety, expectation, fear of making mistakes. It is always seeking control, security, validation. The angelic voice, on the other hand, vibrates at the frequency of unconditional love. It does not carry judgment, criticism, or fear. It only welcomes, guides, and illuminates, without demanding anything in return.

When you receive a message that puts you down, that makes you doubt yourself, or that blames you for something, that message did not come from the angels. It is an echo of your own insecurities, your fears, the critical voices that you have internalized throughout life. Angels do not judge. They do not condemn. They do not punish. They only love. And this loving frequency is perceptible, even when the message is challenging. Because angelic love is not complacency. It is truth, spoken with firmness, but always with compassion.

The third key to discerning is to observe the effect of the message on your field. The mind, when it is guiding the process, tends to generate more noise, more anxiety, more doubts. It fragments, separates, analyzes in excess. The angelic voice, on the other hand, unifies, harmonizes, integrates. It brings a sense of peace, clarity, inner alignment. Even if the message brings a challenge, a call to change or correct something, it does so in a way that makes you feel welcomed and supported, not diminished or criticized.

If, when receiving a message, you feel more tense, more insecure, or more confused, it is important to question the origin of that message. It is possible that it is just a reflection of your own anxieties, or even interference from dense energies that take advantage of your openness to try to confuse you. Angels do not generate fear, nor doubt, nor guilt. They generate light. And this light, even if it reveals your shadows, does so in a way that makes you feel loved and supported, not threatened or abandoned.

With time and practice, you will learn to recognize the vibrational signature of each angel. Each being of light has a unique frequency, a "tone of voice" that resonates in a particular way in your field. Some bring a sweetness that calms the mind, others a firmness that propels you to action. Some manifest as a soft warmth in the chest, others as a fresh breeze that crosses the soul. This signature is their identity, the way they present themselves even before speaking. And, as you become familiar with these presences, the distinction between the inner voice and the angelic voice becomes natural, like recognizing the voice of a dear friend in a crowd.

It is important to remember that the mind is not an enemy of channeling. It is a powerful tool, which can be a great ally in this process. But, for this, it needs to learn to serve the soul, and not to control it. The mind needs to be educated to recognize its own limits, to silence itself when necessary, and to trust the wisdom that comes from the heart. When the mind becomes humble, it becomes a reliable translator of angelic light. It organizes messages, translates intuitions into words, and anchors the experience in the material plane.

Channeling angels is, therefore, an act of inner balance. It is learning to listen with the heart, but to register with the mind. It is trusting intuition, but using discernment. It is opening up to the subtle, but keeping your feet firmly on the ground. And, in this delicate balance, the voice of the angels becomes clear, distinct, unmistakable. Because it is not just a voice you hear—it is a voice you recognize as part of yourself, of your deepest essence, of that part of you that always knew you were never alone.

Over time, this art of listening between the noises becomes a practice of self-knowledge as profound as channeling itself. Because by learning to distinguish what is the voice of the soul, what is the voice of the mind, and what is the angelic whisper, you inevitably encounter your most subtle layers—those that shape your perceptions, your beliefs, and even your resistances. Listening to the angels, in the end, is also learning to listen to yourself from a quieter, truer place, where essence and the divine touch.

Therefore, the true difference between the inner voice and the angelic voice ceases to be a matter of technique and reveals itself as a matter of intimacy. The more intimate your relationship with your angels, the more natural it becomes to recognize them, not only by what they say, but by how they arrive, by the silence they leave, and by the calm certainty that, among all the voices that inhabit your inner world, that one is the only one that carries the exact sound of the love that always accompanies you.

Chapter 21
Trials and Tests of the Channel

Angelic channeling reveals itself as a journey of spiritual maturation, in which the individual, by opening to the connection with subtle planes and the reception of divine messages, is led into a process of deep and irreversible inner refinement. This path is not limited to the passive reception of guidance or the search for communion with beings of light, but implies, above all, the courageous confrontation of one's own internal layers of beliefs, fears, and resistances, which emerge to the surface precisely to be seen, understood, and transcended. Each step in this journey represents a silent invitation for the channel to recognize their hidden strengths and discover within themselves the ability to be an integral and transparent bridge between heaven and earth. The true channel is not born from the absence of challenges but from the courage to face them, transforming each trial into raw material for strengthening their own light and inner clarity.

The refinement of the channel takes place in the invisible field of the soul, where each doubt, each hesitation, and each internal voice of self-sabotage reveals unresolved aspects of the self, echoing old wounds or limiting beliefs that, for a long time, conditioned their perception of their own spirituality and personal worth. The rational mind, accustomed to demanding tangible explanations, confronts the experience of channeling with distrust, which requires the channel to engage in continuous learning to distinguish between the voices of fear and the messages of intuition. This process, far from being an obstacle, is the very essence of spiritual refinement: learning to listen to the subtle even amid internal and external noise, and, above all, learning to trust the truth that resonates in the silence of the soul. Every test that arises, every situation that challenges the channel's faith, functions as a mirror reflecting the degree of their own surrender and trust in divine communication. It is in the act of maintaining the connection even when the ego cries out for guarantees that the channel strengthens, becoming an increasingly clear and distortion-free space for divine guidance.

The external trials that cross this path also play a fundamental role in consolidating the channel's commitment to their own inner truth. Doubts projected by the skeptical gaze of others, circumstances that seemingly divert the channel from their practice or force them to defend their sensitivity in the face of others' incomprehension, all serve as filters that test the solidity of their spiritual choice. It is not about convincing the world around them of the truth of their experiences, but about recognizing, even in moments of greatest challenge, that the strength of the channel does not lie in external recognition, but in the integrity with which they sustain their own connection, regardless of what occurs outside themselves. Each trial, internal or external, when faced with humility and firmness, purifies not only the channel but also the very flow of light that passes through them, making their presence and voice increasingly clear instruments of angelic guidance. It is in this intertwining of challenge and surrender, between purification and spiritual maturity, that the channel recognizes themselves as an essential part of the great network of light that unites the visible to the invisible, learning to walk with serene faith and unshakable trust, even when the path remains shrouded in mist.

These trials are not punishments or spiritual traps. They are, in fact, opportunities for growth, invitations for you to strengthen yourself as a channel and deepen your connection with the angels. Just as the caterpillar needs to break through the cocoon to transform into a butterfly, the channel also needs to cross their internal resistances so that their sensitivity can fully blossom.

One of the first trials to arise is doubt. The human mind, accustomed to the material world and linear logic, struggles to fully trust something that cannot be explained or proven by ordinary senses. When the first messages arrive, the mind questions: "Is this real? Am I just making up what I want to hear?" This doubt is natural and is part of the channel's maturation process.

The angels are not offended by your doubts. They understand them as part of your human nature. But they also expect you to learn to deal with them, to recognize the difference between the voice of insecurity and the voice of intuition. Learning to trust yourself is one of the pillars of channeling.

Another common trial is self-sabotage. Often, without realizing it, the channel places obstacles in their own path. They sabotage themselves, create excuses to avoid dedicating themselves to the practice, or convince themselves that they are not worthy of receiving the angelic presence. This self-sabotage can manifest in various forms—procrastination, fear of exposure, or even the relentless search for external validation.

The root of this self-sabotage often lies in limiting beliefs about oneself. Beliefs that you are not good enough, that you do not deserve the light, or that you are incapable of being a channel. These beliefs are like invisible chains that prevent you from flying. Freeing yourself from them is a process of deep self-knowledge and healing.

The angels love you unconditionally, but they also respect your free will. If you choose to remain trapped by these beliefs, they cannot force you to free yourself. But they remain by your side, patient and loving, waiting for you to recognize your own strength and choose to break these chains.

There are also external trials. People who doubt or mock your journey, situations that seem to conspire against your moments of connection, or even unexpected challenges that test your faith. These trials can be painful, but they are also opportunities to strengthen your conviction.

The angels do not protect you from all of life's difficulties. But they support you during the passage through them. They whisper courage, inspire solutions, and help you see the lesson behind each challenge.

Facing these trials with confidence is a way to show the universe—and yourself—that you are committed to your journey.

It is important to remember that trials are not a sign that you are on the wrong path. On the contrary, they are a sign that you are progressing. If you were not opening yourself to something greater, there would be no resistance. The caterpillar does not need to fight the cocoon if it is not ready to fly.

How you handle these trials defines the strength of your channel. If you retreat in the face of doubt, give in to self-sabotage, or allow yourself to be shaken by external difficulties, you weaken your connection. But if you welcome doubt with compassion, free yourself from the chains of self-sabotage, and face external challenges with faith, you strengthen your bond with the angels and become an even clearer and more powerful channel.

The angels do not abandon you during trials. They watch you with love and respect, ready to support you when you ask for help. But they also expect you to use your own wings, to trust in the strength they have helped awaken in you.

Crossing the trials is like polishing a diamond. Each challenge, each doubt, each moment of self-sabotage overcome removes a layer of impurity, revealing the brilliance of your true essence. And this brilliance, in turn, illuminates your path even more, attracting the angelic presence with greater strength and clarity.

Channeling angels is, therefore, a journey of constant learning. It is learning to trust yourself, to free yourself from limiting beliefs, and to face challenges with faith and courage. It is recognizing that trials are not obstacles, but steps that lift you higher and higher on your journey of connection with the light.

As the channel crosses these trials, something profound and subtle happens within them. Each challenge faced, each doubt embraced and transformed, each moment of courage amid uncertainty gradually carves out a wider and more receptive internal space. This expansion is not only a spiritual refinement but also an internal reorganization that allows the light to flow more freely. The channel becomes, little by little, a clearer mirror of the angelic presence, where the message can reflect without distortion, and the essence of the divine reveals itself with greater clarity.

And when the channel understands that each trial is, in fact, a kind of silent initiation, they learn to walk with greater lightness and confidence. Instead of fearing the tests or doubting their own capacity, they begin to recognize them as inevitable parts of their own blossoming. Discomfort ceases to be seen as a sign of error or inadequacy and comes to be understood as the firm and loving touch that awakens them to layers of themselves that were still waiting to be acknowledged.

The channel matures not through the absence of difficulties, but through the constant choice to remain present and available, even when the path seems foggy. And it is in this sincere willingness, in this silent commitment to being a bridge between worlds, that the angels become even more present. For it is precisely in the heart that crosses its shadows without fleeing that light finds fertile ground to bloom.

Chapter 22
Working with the Circle of Angels

By entering the work with the circle of angels, the channel opens to an experience of spiritual connection that transcends individual interaction with a single being of light and enters an expanded vibrational field, where multiple angelic consciousnesses act in a synergistic and complementary way. This circle is not just a random composition of celestial presences, but a true living and organic structure, carefully adjusted to the vibration, trajectory, and specific evolutionary needs of the one who is willing to serve as a conscious channel of divine light. Each angel that integrates this circle presents itself not only as an external presence, but as a direct emanation of qualities that the channel itself needs to awaken, develop, or polish within themselves. Interacting with the circle of angels is not just a spiritual consultation or a search for answers, but a process of deep resonance, where the light of each angel acts as a mirror and catalyst for the channel to recognize their own latent capacities and their sacred essence in constant remembrance.

This collaborative dynamic between the channel and their circle of angels creates a field of continuous learning, in which each angelic presence acts in perfect harmony with the others, forming a network of vibrational support capable of sustaining the channel in their various phases of growth and transition. Some angels approach with the function of nurturing fragile emotional aspects, others offer clarity and discernment in moments of mental confusion, while others still sustain the spiritual protection necessary for the channel to maintain their energy integrity in the face of external challenges. This circle acts, therefore, as a living expression of divine unity, where each voice, each subtle touch, and each specific orientation adds to the greater symphony of the spiritual purpose of the one who serves as a bridge between the planes. By recognizing the presence of this circle and allowing themselves to be supported by it, the channel abandons the illusion of separation and spiritual isolation, understanding that their journey, although unique in its expression, is sustained by a loving constellation of consciousnesses that share the same purpose of serving the evolution of the whole.

True work with the circle of angels is not limited to the passive reception of messages or the punctual evocation of help in times of crisis. It is a continuous and evolutionary relationship, where the channel is called to develop keen inner listening, refined vibrational sensitivity, and, above all, unwavering trust in the wisdom that flows from these subtle interactions. This trust does not arise from absolute certainty or the complete elimination of doubts, but from the willingness to walk even without all the answers, sustained only by the living memory of the constant presence of this spiritual team. Over time, the circle of angels ceases to be perceived as something external, positioned around the channel, and begins to be recognized as a natural extension of their own multidimensional soul—a vibrational projection of the wisest, most compassionate, and luminous parts of their own being. In this recognition, the channel understands that true communion with the circle of angels is, in essence, a journey of return to their own divine essence, where each angel reflects a forgotten face of who they truly are and have always been.

The circle of angels is not just a group of beings of light gathered by chance. It is a spiritual team, carefully formed to support your journey and your specific purposes. Each angel in this circle carries a quality, a specialty, a frequency that complements the others, creating a web of support that adjusts to your needs and your mission.

Working with a circle of angels is like having access to a personalized spiritual council. Instead of seeking guidance from just one source, you open yourself to the combined wisdom and love of various presences. Each angel contributes with their unique perspective, with their specialty, creating a symphony of support that nurtures your soul on different levels.

This spiritual team is not fixed. It transforms as you evolve and your purposes expand. Some angels remain as constant pillars—your guardian angel, for example, is a lifelong member of your circle. Others may approach for a time, offer their light and wisdom at a specific moment, and then move away, opening space for new presences.

The formation of the circle is not just a matter of randomly calling angels that you admire or know. It is a process of deep listening, of recognizing which qualities you need to cultivate in your life and which angelic presences resonate with these qualities. If you seek to strengthen your courage, Michael will be a powerful ally. If emotional healing is the focus, Raphael and Chamuel will bring their vibrations of love and compassion. If wisdom and mental clarity are what you seek, Jophiel and Uriel will illuminate your path.

Communication with a circle of angels requires sensitivity and practice. In the beginning, it can be challenging to discern between the different presences, recognize which angel is speaking, and interpret the combined messages. But, over time, you will learn to identify each one's vibrational signature, recognize their tones of light, and integrate their messages into a single harmonious guidance.

The circle of angels is not a hierarchy. There is no "chief" angel who commands the others. It is a team of equals, united by the purpose of serving your journey. Each angel contributes with their light, but none of them overlap or diminish the importance of the others.

By working with a circle of angels, you open yourself to a multidimensional support experience. Each angel acts on a specific level of your being—physical, emotional, mental, or spiritual. They communicate with you through different channels—dreams, visions, intuitions, physical sensations. And, by integrating these messages, you realize that you are not just receiving guidance, but being cared for in your entirety.

The circle of angels is an extension of your own spiritual team. In addition to the angels, you can connect with ascended masters, spiritual guides, ancestors of light, and other loving presences that resonate with your journey. This complete team forms an invisible support network, which supports you at every step, guides you in every decision, and reminds you, at every moment, that you are never alone.

Creating a circle of angels is an invitation to trust. It is recognizing that you do not have to carry the weight of the world alone. It is opening yourself to the possibility of being supported, guided, and loved by beings of light who have dedicated their existences to serving the evolution of humanity.

As you connect with your circle of angels, your life transforms into a sacred dance. Every step you take is guided by combined wisdom, every decision is illuminated by collective love, every challenge is crossed with the strength of invisible support. And, by surrendering to this dance, you realize that you are not just channeling angels—you are becoming an angel to yourself.

The circle of angels is a portal to the experience of unity. By connecting with different presences, you recognize that the light that emanates from each of them is the same light that shines in you. And, in this recognition, the separation between you and the divine dissolves, revealing the essential truth: you are part of the same web of light that connects all things.

Working with a circle of angels is, therefore, a path of expansion of consciousness and deepening of connection with the divine. It is recognizing that you are not alone on your journey, that there is a team of light ready to support and guide you towards your highest mission. It is opening yourself to the experience of being loved, cared for, and sustained by a force greater than you, but which, at the same time, is an inseparable part of who you are.

Over time, the relationship with this circle of angels ceases to be just a spiritual practice and begins to intertwine with daily gestures, the most intimate thoughts, and even the silences between one action and another. The angels are not just distant voices that bring answers; they become living presences that accompany every step, offering sustenance even in moments when the connection seems tenuous. And it is in this silent and constant coexistence that true intimacy with the circle is revealed—not as an extraordinary event, but as a subtle current of love and guidance flowing behind ordinary life.

This joint work requires neither perfection nor special gifts; it is born from the sincere willingness to open up, to trust, and to recognize that there is wisdom in the invisible, even when the human mind hesitates to accept. The circle of angels molds itself as the channel grows, not to fit it into a rigid role, but to accompany it in its phases of expansion and recollection. There are times when the presence of the circle is like a vibrant chorus, involving every step with clarity and direction.

At others, it is a delicate whisper, almost imperceptible, asking only that the channel remember: "We are here."

Working with a circle of angels is, above all, learning to belong to yourself and to the web of light that sustains all existence. Each angel, with their unique frequency, reflects a part of who you are, and, by recognizing these presences and welcoming them, you become a mirror of your own divine essence. In this reflection, the path is revealed not as a search for something external, but as a slow and loving reminder that, from the beginning, you were already part of this circle, this light, and this love that never stopped pulsating in you.

Chapter 23
Tuning in with Specific Archangels

The connection with archangels manifests as a process of refining consciousness and vibrational alignment, in which the channel becomes capable of tuning into primordial archetypal forces that sustain the very fabric of creation. These great beings of light, which transcend the figure of celestial messengers to act as living expressions of divine attributes, reveal themselves not only as external spiritual guides, but as luminous mirrors of powers already existing in the core of each soul. Each archangel carries in its essence a pure emanation of qualities that structure the journey of the human soul: courage, healing, wisdom, love, truth, renewal, and protection. By tuning into these presences, the channel not only receives assistance and guidance, but awakens in itself the same forces, recognizing itself as a conscious co-creator of the reality it inhabits and traverses.

The process of tuning in with specific archangels does not occur as an isolated event or a punctual call in moments of need. It is, above all, a path of deep self-knowledge, in which the channel is invited to reflect on which internal aspects clamor for expansion or healing. Each archangel, by responding to the sincere call of the soul, acts as an activator of internal codes, reactivating ancestral memories and opening portals of reconnection with the original matrix of the soul. This attunement does not consist of bringing an external presence inward, but rather of removing layers of forgetfulness and fear, allowing the light of one's own being to reverberate in unison with the archetypal frequency of the invoked archangel. By calling Michael, the channel not only receives protection; it awakens its own inner warrior, the inextinguishable flame of courage and integrity. By tuning in with Raphael, it not only calls for healing; it rediscovers in itself the power to regenerate its wounds, welcoming them as portals of wisdom and compassion.

This vibrational dance between channel and archangel reveals itself, over time, as a two-way street, where the divine presence manifests not to replace or superimpose the autonomy of the channel, but to remind it of its co-creative nature and its active role in the manifestation of divine qualities in the physical world. The archangels do not come as distant saviors, but as loving allies who sustain and mirror the latent power within the growing soul. As the channel deepens its attunement, it perceives that the presence of each archangel is not something separate from itself, but an extension of its own divine essence. Michael, Gabriel, Uriel, Raphael, and the many other archangels are not just sacred names or external forces on high planes; they are internal pulsations, divine aspects of the soul itself which, when recognized, begin to express themselves naturally in everyday thoughts, actions, and choices.

Attunement with specific archangels ceases to be an occasional spiritual practice and becomes integrated into the spiritual identity of the channel, dissolving the separation between human and divine, between channel and messenger, between call and response.

Understanding that each archangel represents an aspect of the channel's own divine essence transforms this relationship into a field of continuous spiritual learning and maturity. The presence of Michael, for example, is not invoked only to ward off external dangers, but to remind the channel of its innate ability to draw sacred boundaries and uphold its truth even in the face of opposing forces. Raphael does not act only to restore the ailing body or mind, but to teach that all true healing is born from the loving embrace of one's shadows and the compassionate integration of each fragmented part of the being. By opening oneself to this conscious and mature attunement, the channel perceives that the light of the archangels does not come from the outside in, but emerges from the inside out, unveiling an essential truth: each human soul, in its innermost core, is a reflection of the divine light that the archangels emanate, and each step of its journey is an opportunity to express, in the visible world, the same light that pulsates eternally in its hidden essence.

Connecting with a specific archangel is like opening a direct channel to the source of that quality you seek to strengthen in your life. If courage is what you need, Michael, the archangel of protection and strength, approaches with his sword of light, dissolving fears and strengthening your determination. If physical or emotional healing is the focus, Raphael, the archangel of healing and compassion, envelops you with his emerald wings, soothing pains and opening space for regeneration.

Each archangel has a unique vibrational signature, a color, a sound, a feeling that differentiates it from the others. By invoking a specific archangel, you are not just calling a distant entity, but adjusting your own energy field to tune into its frequency. It's like turning the dial of a cosmic radio, searching for the station that transmits the music your soul needs to hear.

This attunement does not require complex techniques or mystical knowledge. The archangels respond to the purity of intention and the sincerity of the call. A simple prayer, said with an open heart, is enough to create the vibrational bridge. But it is important to remember that true attunement is not just a mental act. It is a state of being.

To connect with Michael, for example, it is not enough to simply pronounce his name. It is necessary to awaken your own inner courage, to recognize the strength that already exists within you and to be willing to use it to defend your values, your dreams, and your mission. Michael does not fight your battles for you. He reminds you that you already have the sword and shield—and invites you to wield them with confidence.

Similarly, to connect with Raphael, it is not enough to simply ask for physical or emotional healing. It is necessary to open yourself to compassion, to welcome your own pains with gentleness and to recognize that true healing is not just the disappearance of symptoms, but the transformation of the way you relate to them. Raphael does not heal for you. He reminds you that you already have the balm and the light—and invites you to use them to take care of yourself and others.

Each archangel is a master in their area of expertise. Uriel, the archangel of wisdom, illuminates your mind with the golden flame of clarity, helping to dissolve doubts and find creative solutions to life's challenges. Gabriel, the messenger, strengthens your inner voice, inspiring authentic communication and the expression of your truth. Chamuel, the archangel of unconditional love, opens your heart to compassion, kindness, and forgiveness, helping to dissolve resentments and build more harmonious relationships.

Attunement with a specific archangel is not a relationship of dependence. The archangels do not want followers or devotees. They want you to recognize your own strength, your own light, your own ability to express the divine qualities they represent. They are like loving teachers, who point the way, but expect you to take the steps on your own legs.

This attunement is also not exclusive. You can connect with different archangels throughout your life, as your needs and purposes evolve. In moments of fear, Michael is the guardian you call. In moments of pain, Raphael is the healer who approaches. And in moments of seeking wisdom, Uriel is the master who illuminates.

The archangels do not compete with each other. They work together, like a cosmic team that serves the evolution of humanity. Each of them contributes with their light, their strength, their wisdom, creating an invisible web of support that supports every step of your journey.

By connecting with a specific archangel, you are not just receiving external help. You are awakening a part of yourself that resonates with that divine quality. It's like activating a dormant code in your spiritual DNA, which connects you to the source of courage, healing, wisdom, or love.

This attunement is a vibrational dance. You adjust your field, and the archangel responds, approaching with their light and guidance. It is a subtle dialogue, which takes place on different levels of perception—dreams, intuitions, synchronicities, physical sensations. Learning to recognize this language is part of the channel's maturation process.

Over time, you will realize that attunement with the archangels is not just a spiritual practice. It is a way of living. You become a permanent channel of those divine qualities that you have chosen to strengthen in yourself. And, by expressing them in your life, you become a beacon for others, inspiring and illuminating the path of those who are still seeking their own light.

Connecting with the archangels is, therefore, an invitation to the expansion of consciousness and the remembrance of your true nature. It is recognizing that you are not alone on your journey, that there are powerful and loving beings of light ready to support and guide you towards your highest mission. It is opening yourself to the experience of being loved, cared for, and sustained by a force greater than you, but which, at the same time, is an inseparable part of who you are.

As this attunement deepens, the channel begins to perceive that each archangel, with their light and purpose, is not a distant or unreachable presence, but an extension of the very divine that dwells in their being. Michael, Raphael, Uriel, Gabriel, and so many others cease to be just names or sacred images and become living pulsations within one's own heart, vibrant echoes of qualities that have always been there, waiting for the right moment to awaken. With each encounter, the channel not only receives a blessing or guidance—it remembers, little by little, who it really is.

This memory is the true gift of attunement with the archangels. More than immediate answers or solutions, they offer a mirror where the channel can see their strength reflected, their wisdom intuited, their love expanded. Each invocation is, in fact, a call inward, a deep dive into the luminous waters of one's own essence. In this continuous flow between receiving and recognizing, between welcoming and expressing, that the channel understands that the divine is not something to be reached, but something to be revealed — layer by layer, breath by breath.

Over time, attunement with the archangels becomes more than a conscious act; it transforms into a constant presence, a silent companionship that permeates the days and nights, the moments of prayer and everyday gestures. Each step, each choice, and each silence carries the subtle mark of these loving presences. And, by living in this way, the channel understands that being guided by the archangels does not mean depending on their light, but learning to recognize that same light pulsing, eternally alive, within oneself.

Chapter 24
Channeling Angelic Names and Seals

Channeling angelic names and seals represents a natural refinement of the channel's spiritual sensitivity, an unfolding that occurs when the connection with the angelic plane reaches a depth where common words can no longer translate the essence of communication. Angelic names, far from being mere identifiers, are condensed vibrational expressions, where each sound carries a specific frequency capable of opening internal and external portals of direct connection with the consciousness of that being of light. Upon receiving a name, the channel is not merely obtaining a way to call or invoke the angelic presence; they are being gifted with a vibrational fragment of that angel's essence, a sonic key capable of attuning their energy field to the exact frequency of the one who presents themselves. These names, when vocalized, thought, or written, function as spiritual memory triggers, recalling not only the angel's identity but the very memory of the ancestral bond between the soul and the angelic presence, which often dates back to cycles far preceding the current incarnation.

This revelation of names does not occur randomly or linearly, but rather as the channel shows readiness to sustain this vibration in their own field. Each name carries a spiritual responsibility, as it evokes a specific frequency of which the channel becomes the guardian and transmitter. Therefore, the process of receiving these names is always surrounded by an atmosphere of deep respect and reverence, as each name is an invitation to integrate specific qualities that the angel represents. More than a sound, the name is a living vibration that interacts directly with the channel's subtle bodies, adjusting, amplifying, and refining their own frequency to make them increasingly capable of sustaining the angelic presence in its totality. This gradual integration causes, in many cases, the revealed name to resonate not just as something external, but as an internal memory, as if the soul recognizes in that sacred sound a forgotten part of itself, reactivated by the encounter.

Angelic seals, in turn, are visual languages of the same vibrational essence contained in the names. If the name is the sonic expression of an angel's signature, the seal is its geometric expression. Each stroke, each curve, and each point of an angelic seal has a reason for being, functioning as a symbolic bridge between the physical plane and the angelic plane. When channeling a seal, the channel is capturing not just a symbol, but a vibrational configuration capable of anchoring the presence of that angel in the material plane. Just as with names, the process of channeling seals is deeply intuitive and occurs when the channel aligns sufficiently with the angel's frequency to capture their emanations in the form of geometric or pictographic symbols. These seals can manifest spontaneously, as visions in meditation, or can be transmitted through automatic writing or creative impulses that flow without the interference of the rational mind.

More than mere decorative or identifying elements, these seals carry a specific vibrational function. They act as anchors of presence, graphic portals that adjust the energy field of the environment and the channel themselves, facilitating communication and stabilizing the frequency of the angelic presence. Each time a seal is consciously drawn or visualized, the channel reinforces the vibrational bridge between the worlds, strengthening their ability to sustain the angelic presence in the physical plane. The process of receiving and working with names and seals becomes a practice of spiritual co-creation, where the channel not only receives information but becomes an active participant in building a sacred field of connection. By integrating these names and seals into their daily practice, the channel transforms into a guardian of these vibrational keys, awakening in themselves and in the world around them the frequencies that these symbols carry, and allowing angelic light to permeate all aspects of their journey with increasing awareness.

Angelic names are not mere labels or titles. They are, in essence, vibrational signatures, light codes that contain the unique frequency of each being of light. Unlike human names, which serve to identify and differentiate, angelic names are access portals to the very essence of the angel. Upon receiving an angelic name, you are not just learning how to call that being—

you are receiving a key to access their frequency, their mission, and their purpose in the universe.

These names can be channeled in various ways. Some arise spontaneously during meditation, as if whispered into your inner ear. Others reveal themselves in dreams, written in light or carved into dreamlike landscapes. There are cases where the name is transmitted through inspired writing, where the hand moves guided by an invisible force, tracing letters and symbols that form an unknown name, but one that resonates with the soul as an ancestral memory.

Channeling angelic names is not a gift reserved for a few. Anyone who cultivates openness, purity of intention, and trust in the loving presence of angels can receive this gift. However, it is necessary to be prepared to deal with the rational mind, which often questions the validity of what was received. Doubt is natural, but it should not be an obstacle. The true test of the authenticity of a channeled name is the resonance it provokes within you. If the name vibrates in your heart, if it awakens a feeling of recognition and deep connection, then it is true, regardless of any external validation.

Angelic seals, in turn, are sacred symbols, vibrational imprints that contain the energetic signature of each angel. They are like coded keys, which open specific portals in your field and allow you to access that angel's frequency more easily and clearly. Unlike names, which are received mainly through inner hearing or inspired writing, angelic seals manifest more frequently through vision. They can appear as clear images, as flashes of light, or as complex geometric designs that form on the screen of your mind during meditation.

Like names, angelic seals are not just beautiful shapes or random designs. Each stroke, each curve, each symbol contained in a seal carries a specific frequency. By meditating on a seal, by drawing it or visualizing it, you are attuning your field with the vibration of that angel, opening yourself to receive their light, their protection, and their guidance.

It is important to remember that channeling angelic names and seals is not an end in itself. It is a powerful tool to strengthen your connection with angels, to deepen your understanding of the language of light, and to open yourself to new layers of perception. However, the true power of these symbols does not reside in their external form, but in the resonance they awaken within you. If a name or seal does not vibrate in your heart, if it does not evoke a feeling of deep connection, then it is not a true key for your journey.

Channeling angelic names and seals is an important step in the channel's journey. It marks a new stage in communication with angels, where language becomes more subtle, deeper, and more personal. By opening yourself to this form of communication, you are opening yourself to a new dimension of your own spirituality, where the connection with angels becomes more intimate, more present, and more integrated into your life as a whole.

It is essential to remember that angels do not reveal their names and seals to satisfy the curiosity of the mind. They do so to strengthen the bond, to deepen trust, and to remind you that you are never alone. Each name, each seal is a gift, a gesture of love that invites you to approach, to recognize the constant presence, and to open yourself to the experience of being guided, supported, and loved by beings of light who have dedicated their existences to serving the evolution of humanity.

Over time, the channel understands that names and seals are not just identification elements, but living bridges between worlds. They carry in their frequencies the very essence of the angelic presence, as if each stroke and each sound vibrated in harmony with the music of that angel's spirit. They are more than access codes—they are silent invitations for the channel to recognize their own ability to hear the subtle, to see beyond form, and to translate into symbols what the soul already knows, but the mind is still learning to decipher.

Each name received, each seal drawn or glimpsed in meditation, is a piece of a larger map—a map that reveals not only the path of connection with angels, but also the channel's own journey towards their luminous essence. These vibrational fragments fit into the flow of the spiritual journey like pieces of a sacred puzzle, where the true purpose is not to decipher or possess the names and seals, but to allow them to transform you, that each revealed frequency opens a new space within you for light to dwell.

The channel discovers that the true key has never been outside—not in the names, nor in the seals, nor in the visions that arise in silence. The true key has always been the willingness to open up, to trust, and to remember that this language of light is not foreign to the soul. On the contrary, it is the mother tongue of the spirit, echoing since the beginning of time and waiting, patiently, for the channel to remember that each name they receive and each symbol they trace are not just invitations to know the angels, but invitations to remember oneself.

Chapter 25
Sounds and Frequency Codes

Communication with angels expands beyond words and mental images, delving into a vibrational dimension where the essence of each message is expressed as pure sound and pulsation. Sounds and frequency codes constitute this primordial language, preceding form and interpretation, a stream of pure vibration that resonates directly in the subtle bodies and the channel's energy field. More than mere sound stimuli, these frequencies are bearers of divine intelligence, imbued with information that does not need to be rationally understood to fulfill its function of harmonizing, unblocking, and awakening hidden aspects of consciousness. Each sound or code received is a living bridge between the human plane and the angelic spheres, capable of adjusting the channel's vibrational field so that it becomes increasingly receptive to the presence and guidance of beings of light.

During the channeling process, these frequencies can manifest in different ways, according to the sensitivity and vibrational configuration of each channel. In some cases, the sounds arrive as delicate melodies, subtle harmonies that echo internally like an ancestral song, bringing with them a sense of welcome and belonging. For others, these sounds may appear as rhythmic pulsations, soft beats that accompany breathing or blood flow, as if the body itself transformed into an instrument that responds to the angelic presence. There are also those who perceive the sounds as isolated fragments, such as crystalline bells, metallic buzzing, or continuous vibrations, each containing a specific vibrational key that adjusts to an ongoing need or process. These sounds are not just passive messages — they interact with the channel's field, promoting cleansings, realignments, and activations as the frequency of each one is welcomed and integrated.

Frequency codes, in turn, are visual, auditory, or kinesthetic manifestations of more complex vibrational patterns, which condense and organize spiritual information into a multidimensional symbolic language. When a channel receives a code, whether in the form of a numerical sequence, sacred geometry, or rhythmic patterns, it is being presented with a vibrational matrix that acts directly on the rearrangement of its own internal structures. Each code is a kind of vibrational password, a unique combination of frequencies that, when recognized and assimilated, unlocks layers of spiritual memory, activates dormant potentials, and repositions the channel in its original flow of connection with divine consciousness. The process of decoding these symbols rarely happens in a linear or immediate way, as they operate at deep levels of consciousness, where the rational mind has little access. Instead of direct answers, these codes bring subtle changes in perception, significant synchronicities, and internal reorientations that, little by little, reveal their true meaning.

As the channel develops its sensitivity to capture and integrate sounds and frequency codes, its own presence becomes a resonant field, capable of radiating the angelic frequencies it receives. It ceases to be just a passive receiver of messages and becomes a living bridge between worlds, continually adjusting its own energy field to serve as a transmission channel for these vibrations to its surroundings. The sounds and codes received are not personal properties, but universal expressions of harmony and healing, destined to be shared with the collective through the channel's simple presence. Each time the channel welcomes a new frequency, it adjusts its own vibrational field and, in doing so, contributes to the elevation of the vibration of the environment and the people it interacts with. Tthe frequency language of angels is not just a tool for individual communication, but a continuous flow of service and co-creation, where each sound and each code received integrates the channel into a larger symphony — the living symphony of divine creation in constant expansion.

Angels are, in essence, beings of pure vibration. They exist in realms where light and sound intertwine, forming complex patterns of energy that sustain and harmonize creation. When they communicate with us, they do not just transmit information — they transmit frequencies. And these frequencies, in turn, resonate in our energy field, adjusting our vibration, dissolving blockages, and awakening dormant potentials.

Sounds and frequency codes are the primordial language of angels. They are the basis of communication that precedes words, images, and even sensations. They are the pure vibration that resonates in every cell of your body, in every particle of your energy field.

These sounds can manifest in various ways during channeling. Some channels hear angelic melodies, celestial harmonies that seem to come from a place beyond space and time. Others hear more subtle sounds — crystalline bells, soft buzzing, the rustling of invisible wings. Some perceive these sounds as internal vibrations, as if the body itself were transforming into a musical instrument.

These sounds are not just "music to the ears." They are light codes, frequencies carefully adjusted to activate specific parts of your being. Each sound, each melody, each vibration carries an energy signature that resonates at different levels — physical, emotional, mental, or spiritual.

Some angelic sounds bring healing. They dissolve energy blockages, calm turbulent emotions, and make room for cellular regeneration. Other sounds bring mental clarity, dissolving the fog of doubt and expanding your capacity for perception. There are sounds that awaken intuition, strengthen the connection with your soul, and open you to the experience of unity with the divine.

Frequency codes, in turn, are more complex vibrational patterns. They are like numerical, geometric, or sound sequences that contain specific information, as if they were encoded messages. These codes can be received in different ways — as numerical sequences that appear in dreams or meditations, as geometric designs that form on the screen of your mind, or as melodies that repeat with subtle variations.

Decoding these codes is a process that requires patience and sensitivity. The rational mind, accustomed to linear logic, may try to force an immediate interpretation. But the true understanding of frequency codes happens in layers, through intuition, synchronicity, and attentive observation of your own dreams and feelings.

Each code is like a key that opens a specific door within you. By meditating on a code, by drawing it, or by listening to it repeatedly, you are tuning your field with the frequency it contains. And this tuning, in turn, activates dormant potentials, dissolves blockages, and opens you to new layers of perception.

It is important to remember that sounds and frequency codes are not magical elements that control angels or force channeling. They are harmonization tools, invitations for you to adjust your vibration and open yourself to communication with the divine. Angels do not need you to invoke them with sounds or codes — they respond to the purity of your intention and the sincerity of your call.

However, these sounds and codes are powerful gifts. They are like vibrational shortcuts, which facilitate connection, deepen communication, and accelerate the process of healing and transformation. By opening yourself to this subtle language, you are opening yourself to a new dimension of your own spirituality, where connection with angels becomes more present, more natural, and more integrated into your life as a whole.

With time and practice, you will learn to recognize sounds and frequency codes as part of your daily communication with angels. You will realize that they do not manifest only in moments of meditation or formal channeling — they are present in the sounds of nature, in the melodies that touch your heart, in the patterns that repeat around you.

Learning to listen to this subtle language is like tuning your senses to a new reality, where the music of creation becomes audible. It is recognizing that you are not separate from the flow of life, but that you are an integral part of the cosmic symphony that vibrates in every atom, in every cell, in every particle of the universe.

As this listening deepens, the channel discovers that sounds and codes are not just external manifestations brought by angels — they echo from inside out, like echoes of a spiritual memory that has always existed. Each sound that resonates in the field, each sequence that reveals itself in images or subtle pulsations, is also a reflection of the soul itself in the process of remembrance. The tuning with these codes is, in fact, the remembrance that the body, mind, and spirit already possess, from the origin, the ability to vibrate in harmony with the divine.

This perception transforms the practice of channeling into something that transcends the search for messages or answers. The channel ceases to be just a receiver and becomes a conscious emitter, adjusting its own frequencies, allowing its presence to become, by itself, a vibrational bridge between the visible and invisible realms. Sounds and codes cease to be just sporadic phenomena and begin to compose the invisible track that sustains every moment of its journey, guiding it not only in communication with angels, but in its very way of existing in the world.

The channel understands that each subtle sound, each code received, is part of a larger score — a sacred song that connects its essence to the primordial source from which everything emanates. And by recognizing itself as part of this living symphony, it not only listens to the angels, but learns to sing with them, becoming an active part of the chorus of light that, from the beginning, sustains and cradles creation.

Chapter 26
The Channel's Mission

Angelic channeling represents a profound calling, which transcends the simple reception of spiritual messages and transforms into a journey of self-discovery and service to the sacred. This mission, which emerges from the encounter between the channel's soul and the subtle spheres of the celestial hierarchy, does not impose itself abruptly or externally, but blossoms organically, from the awakening of consciousness and the opening to the constant flow of love and wisdom that permeates the universe. Each channel is, in essence, a convergence point between the visible and the invisible, a living bridge that allows the manifestation of the angelic presence in matter, translating divine impulses into actions, words, and vibrations that touch humanity and the Earth in varied ways. This mission is inseparable from the channel's own essence, as it is born from their greater soul purpose, echoing their inner truth and genuine desire to participate in the great movement of collective healing and elevation. More than a specific function or a role to play, the channel's mission reveals itself as a constant invitation to alignment between their deepest being and the luminous current that flows directly from the heart of the Creator.

Being a conscious channel implies understanding that the mission is not limited to communication with angels, but unfolds in all areas of life, permeating relationships, choices, and creative expressions. Each personal talent, skill, or gift becomes a divine tool at the service of the greater purpose, and the channel learns to recognize their life as part of an invisible network of light, where each gesture of love reverberates throughout creation. The mission, therefore, is neither static nor predefined, but malleable as water, molding itself to circumstances, to the phases of the evolutionary journey, and to the constant flow of inspiration that angels offer. For some, the mission is expressed in silent healings; for others, in written or spoken words that awaken consciousness; for many, it is revealed in daily acts, in casual encounters, and in the way the channel positions themselves before the world — with presence, lovingness, and surrender. Regardless of the form, the essence remains the same: to be a conscious vehicle of divine light, allowing the compassion, wisdom, and beauty of the angelic realm to flow freely through their existence.

Assuming this mission does not mean carrying the weight of unrealistic expectations or seeking unattainable perfection. On the contrary, the true strength of the channel lies in their sacred vulnerability, in the willingness to be transparent enough for light to pass through them without distortions. This process requires courage to look at one's own shadows, accepting one's humanity with tenderness and compassion, for it is precisely in the encounter between light and shadow that the channel becomes whole and able to serve with authenticity. The channel's mission is, above all, an inner experience, a silent commitment to make space for divinity to express itself in the simplicity of everyday life. Each loving choice, each inspired word, and each sincere gesture of care are manifestations of this mission, which is not realized as a distant goal, but as a continuous dance between being and giving, between receiving and sharing, between hearing the voice of angels and translating that celestial melody into service to others. By understanding that their presence is, in itself, an expression of light, the channel discovers that their mission is inseparable from their own essence — a divine flame that burns in the center of their chest and illuminates the path, inside and out, in heaven and on Earth.

Being a conscious angelic channel is not just about receiving messages or having extraordinary spiritual experiences. It is, above all, a call to serve, to be a beacon of light in a world that has often forgotten its own divine essence. It is becoming an instrument of light, allowing the wisdom and love of angels to flow through you to touch the lives of other people and the planet as a whole.

This mission is not an obligation imposed by angels, nor a burden that you need to carry. It is, in fact, a privilege, an opportunity to express your true nature and to contribute to the healing and evolution of humanity. It is a call to share the light you have received, to be a point of connection between heaven and earth, to be an agent of transformation in a world that cries out for love and compassion.

The channel's mission manifests in different ways, according to their talents, skills, and their own soul journey. For some, the mission is expressed through healing — whether through the laying on of hands, the channeling of subtle energies, or the use of words and messages that bring relief and comfort. For others, the mission manifests through art — whether through music, painting, writing, or any form of creative expression that channels the beauty and inspiration of the angelic realm.

There are those whose mission is expressed through teaching — whether through lectures, courses, or books that share the wisdom and knowledge received from the angels. And there are those whose mission is expressed through direct service to the community — whether through volunteer work, social projects, or any form of action that contributes to the well-being of others.

The channel's mission is not something you need to discover alone. The angels guide you, inspire you, and support you every step of the way. They whisper ideas, open doors, and connect you with the right people and resources so that you can express your mission in the most authentic and powerful way possible.

However, it is important to remember that the channel's mission is not something you need to perform perfectly. Angels do not expect you to be an infallible guru or a savior of humanity. They expect you to give yourself sincerely, to share the light you have received with humility, and to trust in the wisdom and love that flow through you.

The channel's mission is not about perfection, but about presence. It is about being present in every moment, in every encounter, in every word and gesture, allowing the light of angels to express itself through you in the most authentic and loving way possible. It is about being an open and receptive channel, trusting that the wisdom and love that flow through you will touch and transform the lives of everyone who crosses your path.

The channel's mission is not something you need to accomplish in the future. It is happening now, in every choice you make, in every word you speak, in every gesture of love and compassion you offer to the world. It is about living your life as an act of service, as an expression of the light you have received, as a manifestation of the love that you are.

This mission intertwines with the soul's own journey, shaping itself to its cycles of growth, to the unfolding learnings, and to the transformations that life invites you to carry out. It is neither a distant goal, nor a fixed destination; it is a constant flow between giving and receiving, between the silence that welcomes and the voice that shares. The channel does not need to have all the answers, nor carry the illusion of always being ready. Their true strength lies in the willingness to open up, to be vulnerable before the light, and to allow their own humanity to walk hand in hand with the divinity that inhabits them.

By accepting this mission, the channel learns to dance between the visible and the invisible, between the sacred and the everyday. Each experience, however simple it may seem, becomes a fertile ground for the angelic presence to manifest — in a welcoming look, in a comforting word, in the silence that listens without haste. It is thus, in small gestures and in great surrenders, that the mission is fulfilled: not as a fixed script, but as a symphony that is composed each day, to the rhythm of the heart and the breath of divine inspiration.

The channel discovers that their mission is, first and foremost, a way of remembering who they truly are. It is the return to the inner home, to the luminous source that has always been present, waiting for the moment to overflow. Each step, each sharing, and each connection becomes a portal to this reunion, in which serving is loving, receiving is giving, and being a channel is, in essence, being whole — a fragment of heaven walking on earth.

Chapter 27
The First Complete Channeling

The first complete channeling represents a moment of profound fusion between the human and the sacred, a silent crossing towards the luminous essence that has always inhabited your being, patiently awaiting permission to express itself. It is not just a spiritual exercise or a technique to be learned, but a true rite of passage in which you, for the first time, recognize yourself as an active part of a current of love and wisdom that flows directly from the angelic plane to your heart. This encounter does not arise from haste or the expectation of immediate results, but from the delicate construction of mutual trust between you and the loving presences that have accompanied you since before your birth. Each conscious breath, each welcomed silence, and each sincere intention pave the way to this moment when the veil between worlds becomes so thin that the voice of the soul can be heard with clarity and tenderness. There are no demands for perfection, nor any need for control over what will be said, felt, or revealed. The first complete channeling is, above all, an internal permission, an absolute yes to the presence of light in your life, allowing it to envelop you, guide you, and transform you from the inside out.

The preparation for this first surrender is not limited to the physical environment or the external ritual, although these elements help to create a field of welcome and safety. True preparation happens in the depths of your being, in the intimate space where your vulnerabilities, your desires, and your doubts meet your faith, your courage, and your desire to serve the light. Each choice of silence amidst the noise, each moment of conscious connection with your heart, and each small act of trust in the gentle voice of your intuition are silent invitations for the angels to approach, not as external forces, but as extensions of the very divine essence that pulses in your chest. This inaugural channeling is less about hearing specific messages and more about remembering the primordial language of the soul—a language made of subtle vibrations, delicate sensations, and perceptions that cannot be completely translated into words. In this sacred space of reunion, the guardian angel is not a distant entity transmitting commands, but an amplified reflection of your own divine spark, a luminous mirror where you can recognize the original brilliance that has always been present, behind the layers of fear, doubt, or self-sabotage.

The flow of this first channeling does not follow a linear script or a predefined sequence of steps, because each soul builds its communication bridge in a unique and unrepeatable way. Some will feel subtle warmth or chills, while others will perceive images, loose words, or just a loving presence that envelops and calms them. No experience is more valid or profound than another, as they all reflect the degree of openness and trust you allow at that moment. More than results, the angels observe the sincerity of your surrender, the pure desire to serve the light, and the courage to open yourself to something greater than the rational mind can comprehend. This first full connection does not end when you conclude the moment of silence; it reverberates in invisible layers of your consciousness, imbuing your gaze, your words, and your gestures with a new quality of presence and lovingness. From it, the separation between spirituality and everyday life dissolves, and you begin to perceive that every moment is an extension of the channeling—every word of comfort you offer, every silence you respect, and every act of compassion you practice becomes a concrete manifestation of the angelic light flowing through you, with or without words, with or without ceremonies. In this sense, the first complete channeling is not an isolated event, but the inaugural milestone of a continuous dance between your humanity and your divine essence, where each step, however simple it may seem, is a silent celebration of the reunion between heaven and earth within you.

This first channeling is not a test, nor a proof that you are ready or not to be a channel. It is, above all, a gift that you offer yourself—a moment of profound connection with your soul and with the wisdom and love that emanate from the celestial spheres. It is a dive into your own inner sea, guided by the gentle hand of your guardian angel, who leads you safely and tenderly through the waves of your own consciousness.

Before starting the channeling, set aside some time to prepare yourself. Choose a moment when you can be at peace, without interruptions or distractions. Turn off your cell phone, television, computer—any device that might divert your attention from the present moment. If possible, create a quiet and welcoming environment—light a candle, put on soft music, use an aroma that helps you relax.

This environmental preparation is not a rigid rule. The angels do not demand a perfect setting to manifest. But by taking care of the external space, you are, in fact, preparing the internal space. You are telling your mind and body that this is a special moment, a moment of encounter with the sacred. And this intention, in itself, is already an important step towards connection.

With the environment prepared, sit comfortably in a place where you can keep your spine straight, but relaxed. Close your eyes and breathe deeply a few times. Feel the air entering and leaving your lungs, filling every cell of your body with life and energy. Breathing is the bridge between the physical body and the soul. By breathing consciously, you harmonize these two planes, creating an internal space conducive to channeling.

While breathing, observe your thoughts. Do not try to stop them or control them. Just observe them as one observes clouds passing in the sky. They come and go, bringing images, emotions, memories. But you don't need to cling to them. Just let them pass, like waves that form and dissipate on the surface of the sea.

The mind is a powerful tool, but during channeling, it needs to learn to quiet down. It does not need to be turned off, but placed in the background, like a respectful observer of the dialogue that takes place between your soul and the angels. By silencing the mind, you open space for the subtle voice of your heart to be heard.

With the body relaxed and the mind at peace, bring your attention to your heart. Feel the rhythm of your breath in this center of your chest. Imagine a soft light emanating from your heart, filling your entire body with a feeling of peace and security. This light is your own divine essence, your inner flame that never goes out, even in the most difficult times.

By connecting with this light, you connect with the frequency of love. And love is the primordial language of the angels. They do not speak only in words or images, but in subtle vibrations that resonate directly in your heart. By opening your heart, you open the door for them to communicate with you in the purest and most loving way possible.

With the heart open and receptive, invite your guardian angel to approach. You can do this aloud or just with thought. It doesn't matter the form—what matters is the sincerity of your call. Tell him that you are ready to listen, that you trust in his presence, and that you open yourself to receive the wisdom and love he has to share.

While waiting for the answer, continue breathing calmly and attentively. Do not worry about feeling something specific or receiving a grandiose message. Just trust the process. The angels do not manifest in the same way for everyone. For some, the presence is felt as a gentle warmth in the chest, for others as a cool breeze that envelops the body. For some, the message comes as an inner voice, for others as a symbolic image.

Do not try to control the experience. Just allow yourself to feel. Welcome any sensation, any image, any thought that arises with gentleness and curiosity. Do not judge, do not question, do not try to force an interpretation. Just observe, as one observes a flower blooming in slow motion.

The first channeling is like a delicate encounter. You are opening yourself to a new form of communication, to a language that is not limited to words or images, but that manifests in different levels of perception. Be patient with yourself. Trust in the wisdom of your guardian angel, who will guide you with love and safety through the layers of your own consciousness.

If, at any time, you feel uncomfortable or insecure, ask for the protection of your angel. Remember that you are not alone in this process. He is by your side, supporting you with his invisible wings, guiding you with his light, and whispering words of comfort and encouragement to you.

The first channeling can last a few minutes or a few hours. There is no predefined time. Trust your intuition. When you feel that the moment has come to an end, thank your angel for the presence and shared wisdom. Thank yourself too, for giving yourself this gift, for opening yourself to this new form of connection with the light.

When you open your eyes, do not worry about immediately recording everything that happened. Write down some keywords, some images or sensations that became stronger. But, above all, allow yourself to integrate the experience. Return to your day with the awareness that you are not alone, that there is a loving presence that accompanies you in every step, that guides you with wisdom, and that loves you unconditionally.

This first channeling is just the beginning. It is the first step in a journey of profound connection with the light, of self-knowledge, and of expansion of consciousness. With each new channeling, trust strengthens, communication becomes clearer, and the angelic presence becomes more present in your life.

With time, you'll realize that each channeling is unique, like an intimate dialogue between souls that recognize each other far beyond words. Some messages will come as soft, almost imperceptible whispers, while others will pour out like a river of wisdom and love. Regardless of the form, each encounter will leave a silent mark, a subtle glow in your eyes, and a serene certainty that something profound has been remembered within you—something that doesn't need to be explained, only felt.

This process of opening and surrendering is not limited to the moment of channeling itself, but extends into everyday life. Each conscious breath, each act of kindness, each instant of silence between one thought and another becomes an opportunity to listen, to feel, and to channel the light that flows through you. Little by little, you understand that true channeling doesn't just happen in the sacred space you prepare, but in every gesture, every encounter, and every choice that aligns your soul with the vibration of love.

And so, the first complete channeling transforms into a silent and sacred milestone—not as a point of arrival, but as the gentle opening of a door that has always been there. From it, you will walk with more lightness, more confidence, and more presence, knowing that you don't need to be perfect, nor have all the answers. Just continue, one step at a time, listening to the voice of your heart and allowing the light that dwells within you to express itself in the world, like a silent prayer that echoes beyond time.

Chapter 28
From Channel to Instrument

The transformation of a channel into a true instrument of light happens when the connection with the angelic plane ceases to be an isolated event and becomes a way of existing, a state of continuous presence in which every gesture, thought, and word reflects the light that flows directly from the divine source. More than transmitting messages or receiving celestial guidance, being an instrument is living in harmony with the vibration of love and compassion, allowing this energy to pour through your daily actions and your presence in the world. It is understanding that channeling is not limited to moments of recollection and silence, but permeates every moment of your life — in how you welcome others, in how you listen, speak, create, and serve. The instrument of light is not a being separated from the physical world, but someone who walks between planes, anchoring the wisdom of heaven into matter, making the invisible visible, in a natural and fluid way. Each talent, each learning, and each experience lived along your journey become components of this great divine symphony, in which your soul is both interpreter and composer, translating the voice of angels into loving and conscious service.

Becoming an instrument of light does not imply renouncing your individuality or transforming into an idealized figure of spiritual perfection. On the contrary, the authenticity of the instrument lies precisely in the integration between your humanity and your divine dimension, in the recognition of your vulnerabilities, fears, and uncertainties, without allowing these layers to hide or muffle the brilliance of your essence. It is in this honest encounter with yourself, where light touches shadow with tenderness and respect, that the true strength of the instrument is born: a presence that welcomes without judging, that listens without haste, that guides without imposing, and that serves without expecting recognition. The service of the instrument is often silent, invisible to external eyes, but profoundly transformative for all who come into contact with its energy. Its mission is not to mold itself to external expectations or repeat ready-made formulas, but to allow its expression to be unique, reflecting the singular combination of gifts, history, and purpose that compose your soul. Whether through words, touch, gaze, silence, or art, the instrument channels light spontaneously, without seeking to control or define how this energy should manifest.

The transition from channel to instrument is a gradual process of loving surrender, where the ego learns to make room for the greater wisdom that flows through the heart. There is no rush, no comparisons, as each soul walks this path at its own pace, according to its degree of openness and spiritual maturity. Angels do not demand perfection or heroism; they only ask for sincerity, willingness, and humility to serve as a living bridge between planes. By becoming an instrument, the channel understands that service is not just an act of giving, but also a constant flow of receiving. Each time it puts itself at service, the instrument is nourished by the same light it shares, strengthening its own connection with the source and deepening the understanding of its true spiritual identity. Being an instrument of light is, therefore, a state of continuous communion with the divine, where serving and being served, giving and receiving, guiding and being guided intertwine in an infinite dance of love and reciprocity. It is in this sacred flow that the channel finds its true fulfillment — not in the search for external recognition, but in the deep and silent joy of knowing that, by serving the world, it serves its own soul and honors the divine essence that dwells within.

Being an instrument means going beyond the passive reception of angelic messages. It is integrating the wisdom and love received into your life and using them to serve others, the community, and the planet as a whole. It is placing yourself at the disposal of light, allowing it to flow through you to touch and transform the lives of all who cross your path.

This transformation from channel to instrument does not happen overnight. It is a gradual process of maturation, integration, and surrender. It's like learning to play a musical instrument: in the beginning, the movements are hesitant, the sounds are uncertain, and the melody does not yet flow naturally. But with practice, with dedication, and with love, the music begins to emerge, and the instrument becomes an extension of your own soul.

Likewise, at the beginning of the channeling journey, you may feel insecure, hesitant to share the messages received, afraid of making mistakes or being misunderstood. But as confidence grows and the connection deepens, you realize that you are not alone. Angels guide you, inspire you, and support you every step of the way. They whisper words of encouragement, open doors, and connect you with the right people so you can express your mission in the most authentic and powerful way possible.

Placing yourself at service as an instrument of light does not mean abandoning your individuality or becoming a puppet in the hands of angels. On the contrary, it is using your talents, skills, and your own soul journey to manifest light in the world. It is integrating angelic wisdom with your own essence and expressing it in a unique and creative way.

This expression of service can manifest in various forms, according to your gifts and personal mission. For some, service manifests through healing — whether through the laying on of hands, the channeling of subtle energies, or the use of words and messages that bring relief and comfort. For others, service manifests through art — whether through music, painting, writing, or any form of creative expression that channels the beauty and inspiration of the angelic realm.

There are those whose mission is expressed through teaching — whether through lectures, courses, or books that share the wisdom and knowledge received from angels. And there are those whose mission is expressed through direct service to the community — whether through volunteering, social projects, or any form of action that contributes to the well-being of others.

The way you put yourself at service is not the most important thing. What really matters is the intention, the purity of your heart, and the love you put into each action. Angels do not expect you to be perfect or to perform great feats. They expect you to give yourself sincerely, to share the light you have received with humility, and to trust in the wisdom and love that flows through you.

Remember: you are not alone on this journey. Angels accompany you, guide you, and inspire you every step of the way. Trust your intuition, follow the signs that the Universe sends you, and act with courage and determination. The world needs your light, your compassion, and your wisdom.

By placing yourself at service as an instrument of light, you not only contribute to the healing and transformation of the world, but you also transform yourself. You become a purer, stronger, and more connected channel to your own divine essence. You become a beacon of hope, an agent of healing, and an instrument of peace.

And as you give yourself, as you share the light you have received, you realize that the true reward of service is not in external recognition, but in the deep joy of being an instrument of divine love. It is in the feeling of unity with the whole, in the certainty that you are fulfilling your mission and contributing to the creation of a more luminous and harmonious world.

Exercise: Co-creating Your Service:

Reflection: Set aside a moment of quiet and introspection. Connect with your heart and ask yourself: how can I use my gifts and talents to serve the world? What is my mission? How can I be an instrument of light?

Intuition: Pay attention to the signs that the Universe sends you. Observe synchronicities, dreams, ideas that come into your mind. Follow your intuition, and it will guide you to the right opportunities to put yourself at service.

Action: Act with courage, determination, and confidence. Do not be afraid of making mistakes or being misunderstood. Trust in the wisdom of angels and the strength of your heart.

Sharing: Share the light you have received. Be a beacon of hope for those around you. Offer your love, your compassion, and your wisdom to the world.

Gratitude: Give thanks for the opportunity to serve, for the trust that angels place in you, and for the joy of being an instrument of light.

Message from the Angels:

"Beloved children of light, You are divine instruments, channels of love and wisdom. Embrace your mission with joy and gratitude. Trust in the strength of your heart, the light of your soul, and the wisdom of your path. Put yourselves at the service of the world, and together we will create a brighter future for all! With eternal love".

Chapter 29
Manifesting the Angelic Alliance

Manifesting the angelic alliance on Earth represents the conscious materialization of the sacred connection between your essence and the celestial realm, integrating this invisible union into every aspect of existence. More than isolated moments of meditation or receiving messages, this alliance becomes a guiding thread between your intentions, your actions, and the greater purpose that guides your soul. Each gesture, word, or daily choice is transformed into a tangible reflection of this luminous partnership, dissolving the separation between spirituality and everyday life. The angelic presence, previously perceived only in moments of recollection, now inhabits your breath, your relationships, your attentive gaze to the world around you. This alliance is not something that needs to be forged from scratch, but rather remembered and awakened, for since the first whispers of the soul, even before your incarnation, this union already existed as a silent commitment between you and the angelic forces that sustain your journey.

Being a conscious guardian of this alliance means recognizing that your life, in itself, is an expression of this connection, and that every experience—from the most intense challenges to the most sublime blessings—serves as an opportunity to allow angelic light to manifest through you. Your personal story, your scars, and your victories are not obstacles to this manifestation, but foundations that make your channel more authentic, compassionate, and capable of radiating angelic wisdom in a humanly understandable way. The alliance does not require spiritual perfection or irreproachable conduct; it flourishes precisely when you embrace your vulnerability and offer yourself as a transparent receptacle for the unconditional love of the angels. Your humanity, with all its layers, becomes the sacred space where this partnership strengthens. By ceasing to seek ideal moments to channel and beginning to perceive every instant of life as a living altar, you dissolve the boundaries between the sacred and the common, between prayer and daily act, allowing existence itself to become a celebration of the alliance that unites your soul with the celestial choirs.

The manifestation of this alliance also reveals itself in the way you relate to your mission, your projects, and your dreams. Every talent, every creative inspiration, or sincere desire to serve arises as a reflection of this connection, a silent call for your creations to be impregnated with the light and wisdom of the angels. The act of teaching, creating, healing, or caring for another ceases to be merely a personal expression and becomes a divine service, an extension of the commitment made between you and your spiritual guides. Your gifts and passions become vehicles of this alliance, translating the invisible beauty of the celestial plane into tangible forms. Even your difficulties or apparent limitations can serve as portals for this manifestation, because the angels do not see you through your imperfections, but as a soul perfectly positioned to reflect a unique portion of divine light. Every act of kindness, every word of comfort, and every conscious choice to radiate love in situations of conflict is, in essence, a living reminder of the alliance between the human and the divine. By living this truth, you not only manifest your angelic alliance but invite everyone around you to remember that this same alliance pulsates silently within every heart.

Manifesting your angelic alliance on Earth is going beyond moments of meditation and formal contact. It is making the presence and wisdom of angels an inseparable part of who you are and how you manifest yourself in the world. It's like weaving angelic light into every thread of your reality, creating a tapestry where heaven and earth intertwine in harmony.

This manifestation is not a one-time event, but a continuous process of alignment and integration. It's like learning to dance with your angels, allowing them to guide your steps, inspire your actions, and sustain your choices. It is recognizing that channeling is not just a spiritual practice, but a way of living.

One of the first steps to manifesting your angelic alliance is recognizing that angels are not limited to your moments of meditation or your sacred spaces. They are with you everywhere, at all times. They accompany you at work, in relationships, in the challenges and joys of everyday life.

By remembering this constant presence, you open space for them to participate in your life more actively. You begin to ask for their guidance before making important decisions, to invoke their protection in moments of difficulty, and to thank them for their presence in every small achievement.

This integration of channeling into your daily life is not about following rigid rules or trying to be perfect all the time. It is about living with awareness, with love, and with the certainty that you are never alone. It is about recognizing that every step you take is guided by the wisdom and love of your angels.

Another powerful way to manifest your angelic alliance is through your projects and your soul mission. Angels are not only interested in your personal spiritual development. They also support you in your dreams, in your goals, and in your mission to contribute to the healing and transformation of the world.

By aligning your projects with the wisdom and love of the angels, you not only increase your chances of success, but also transform your actions into instruments of light. You become an agent of healing, a bearer of hope, a co-creator of the reality that manifests the beauty and harmony of the angelic realm in your creations.

This manifestation of your mission can be expressed in various ways, according to your talents, your passions, and your inner calling. If you are an artist, you can use your art to channel the beauty and inspiration of the angels. If you are a teacher, you can share the wisdom and knowledge received to illuminate the minds and hearts of your students. If you are a healer, you can use your hands and your words to channel the loving energy of the angels and promote physical, emotional, and spiritual healing.

It doesn't matter how you choose to manifest your mission. What matters is that it is aligned with your deepest values, your highest dreams, and the calling of your soul. And by surrendering to this mission, you not only contribute to the creation of a more luminous and harmonious world, but you also fulfill yourself as a human being, expressing your true nature and fulfilling the purpose for which you came to Earth.

Manifesting your angelic alliance is also about sharing the light you have received. It's not about preaching or converting, but about radiating the wisdom and love of the angels in your words, your gestures, and your actions. It is about being a living example of the angelic presence, inspiring others to open themselves to the connection with light and to manifest their own soul mission.

This radiation of light is not about self-promotion or seeking recognition. It is about humility, about serving as a beacon that guides others towards their own inner light. It is about recognizing that you are not the source of light, but merely a channel, an instrument that allows it to manifest in the world.

And as you share this light, as you manifest your angelic alliance on Earth, you will realize that channeling is not just a spiritual practice—it is a way of living. It is being present in every moment, in every encounter, in every word and gesture, allowing the light of the angels to express itself through you in the most authentic and loving way possible. It is being an open and receptive channel, trusting that the wisdom and love that flow through you will touch and transform the lives of all who cross your path.

Manifesting this alliance is recognizing that the angelic presence is not an external force separate from who you are, but a natural extension of your own divine essence. It is allowing this presence to flow through your attentive listening and your compassionate gaze, in the simplest and most challenging moments. Every conscious choice, every silence filled with intention, and every gesture impregnated with love become living expressions of this sacred partnership, dissolving the illusion of separation between the divine and the human.

Over time, this alliance ceases to be a spiritual concept and becomes a pulsating reality, an invisible second skin that surrounds and sustains you. Your voice carries echoes of this connection, your hands become an extension of the wings that support you, and your dreams begin to be woven with the same light that inhabits the sky. There is no division between the moment you channel and the moment you live; life itself becomes channeling, and you walk as a living prayer, a reflection of the sacred in motion.

And it is in this fusion between heaven and earth, between presence and surrender, that your angelic alliance is fully revealed. Not as a title or an achievement to flaunt, but as a state of being, where you and the angels become voices of the same song. With each step, you realize that you are not only manifesting this alliance to the world—you are, in fact, allowing the world itself to remember the ancestral alliance that has always existed between the human and the divine, between the soul and heaven.

Epilogue

There are readings that end. We close the book, gather the ideas, and move on. But there are others that merely inaugurate a listening. This is the case. If you've made it this far, something within you is no longer the same. It's not about knowledge that accumulates, but a memory that activates. Channeling angels is not a technique to master; it's a state of being that, once awakened, accompanies you in every gesture, every silence, every sigh.

You have been invited to recognize that you do not walk alone. That your body is a bridge, your soul a portal, and your heart a living antenna, capable of translating the subtle frequency of those who have never left. Each page traversed an aspect of this dance between the visible and the invisible, between heaven and earth, between the human and the divine. But now, with the book closed, it is you who take on the crossing. Words may cease, but the dialogue has only just begun.

The angels that whispered between the lines, that slipped between the pages and hid in your own feelings as you read, are not just distant beings. They are parts of you. Expressions of your own light, of your own cosmic history. Channeling them is, in essence, remembering. Remembering that every intuition, every hunch, and every moment of sudden peace has always been an ongoing conversation. The veil between you and them has never been solid. It is made of fear, doubt, and forgetfulness. Now, however, you know.

Breathe. Listen to the silence. In the spaces between the noises of the world, there is an ancestral song. A melody of invisible wings, whose chords echo from the first pulse of your spiritual heart. You are the bridge. You are the answer. You are the earthly extension of the celestial light that inhabits the angels.

May this book not end in your hands. May it transform into presence. Into certainty. Into a living memory that your connection has never depended on complex techniques or special gifts. It has always been your birthright.

Live this truth. And the angels will come—because, deep down, they have always been here.

www.ingramcontent.com/pod-product-compliance
Lightning Source LLC
LaVergne TN
LVHW040051080526
838202LV00045B/3577